THE WAY WE WERE IN
SAN DIEGO

THE WAY WE WERE IN

SAN DIEGO

Richard W. Crawford

THE
History
PRESS

Published by The History Press
Charleston, SC 29403
www.historypress.net

Front Cover, top: Horton Plaza on D Street, *bottom:* San Diego Bay looking toward Point Loma;
back cover, bottom: Fifth Avenue. *All postcards courtesy of Special Collections, San Diego Public Library.*

First published 2011
Second printing 2013

Manufactured in the United States

ISBN 978.1.60949.441.4

Library of Congress Cataloging-in-Publication Data

Crawford, Richard W. (Richard William)
The way we were in San Diego / Richard W. Crawford.
p. cm.
"A collection of articles about the history of San Diego from Richard W. Crawford's
local history column "The Way We Were" published in the San Diego Union-Tribune"--
Publisher.
Includes index.
ISBN 978-1-60949-441-4
1. San Diego (Calif.)--History. 2. San Diego (Calif.)--Social life and customs. 3. San Diego
(Calif.)--Biography. I. San Diego union-tribune. II. Title.
F869.S22C74 2011
979.4'985--dc23
2011037320

CONTENTS

CONTENTS

PREFACE

In January 2008, the *San Diego Union-Tribune* began a new weekly feature for its readers: a local history column called "The Way We Were." I began writing this column for the metro edition of the *UT*, while other authors wrote history articles for different regional editions of the newspaper. My first column—written in a year of severe drought—was a piece on the notorious "Rainmaker" Charles Hatfield, remembered as the "creator" of the record rains and floods of January 1916. More articles followed each week, all intentionally varied in subject matter and chronology and always based on historical research. Eventually, the geographical scope of the articles would extend to all of San Diego County.

This book is a selection from the nearly 160 history articles written for the *Union-Tribune* in the last three and a half years. Many of these stories are longer than the original newspaper versions, which were often edited for length. New photographs have also been added for this book edition. I hope that my notes on sources, which conclude the book, will lead readers to more material on the fascinating stories of San Diego history.

ACKNOWLEDGEMENTS

The San Diego community is filled with avid students of our region's history. Many of these friends and colleagues have contributed to my work over the years by their suggestions, encouragement and criticism. I would like to say thanks to my friend and mentor Bud McKanna, history lecturer at San Diego State University; historian Richard Carrico, to whom I am indebted for his successful suggestion of a publisher; *San Diego Union-Tribune* writers and editors, past and present, Welton Jones, Roger Showley, David Ogul, Susan Gembrowski and David Gaddis Smith; archivists Carol Myers and Jane Kenealy at the San Diego History Center; librarian Janet Liggett at San Diego County Law Library; archivist Linda Johnson and the staff at the California State Archives; librarian Mary Allely from the National City Public Library; and the staff of the microform center of the San Diego State University Library.

Friends and institutions have also generously provided historical photographs for the newspaper column and now for this book. I am very grateful for this help from Alan Renga at the San Diego Air & Space Museum, Kevin Sheehan at the Maritime Museum of San Diego, Jeff Pasek at the Water Department of San Diego Public Utilities, the staff of Special Collections at the San Diego Public Library, Mary Shepardson from the Del Mar Thoroughbred Club; and Steve Willard and Rick Carlson from the San Diego Police Museum. Corey Braun and Terry Chaffee provided family photographs, and baseball historian Bill Swank and Chargers historian Todd Tobias loaned images of San Diego sports. Finally, a very heartfelt thank-

ACKNOWLEDGEMENTS

you to Sarah and Ethan, who have tolerated the long workdays from Dad, and for my wife, Susan, for her patience and her critical, candid readings of my stories from San Diego history.

A Frontier Port

The Battle of San Diego Bay

San Diego is a very fine, secure harbour…within there is safe anchorage for ships of any burthen. There is a sorry battery of eight pounders at the entrance: at present, it does not merit the least consideration as a fortification.
— *William Shaler, captain of the American trading ship* Lelia Byrd

In the first years of the 1800s, San Diego's fine harbor offered a welcome respite for the "Boston men"—New England traders who cruised the coast of Spanish-controlled California pursuing the lucrative sea otter fur trade. Guarded only by the small Fort Guijarros at Ballast Point on Point Loma, the harbor was a prized locale for fresh food and water.

Provisions were not the only reason for anchoring in San Diego. The opportunity for smuggling otter pelts was a powerful incentive. All along California's coast, the Boston men were collecting furs—by any means possible—while the Spanish authorities tried to monopolize the selling and keep the profits at home.

The first American trading ship to challenge Spanish authority was the *Alexander*, which entered San Diego in February 1803. Captain John Brown received permission to buy provisions for his scurvy-ridden crew. But while Brown's "sick" sailors recuperated on shore, the captain eagerly bought contraband furs from Indians and soldiers. When the Spanish commandant

This painting by Jerry MacMullen depicts the American brig *Lelia Byrd* fleeing from San Diego Bay under cannon fire from Fort Guijarros at Ballast Point. *Courtesy of Maritime Museum of San Diego.*

got wind of the smuggling, he boarded the *Alexander*, confiscated 491 otter pelts and ordered Brown to leave San Diego immediately.

Two weeks later, on March 17, Captain William Shaler's brig *Lelia Byrd* anchored in San Diego bay. This time the commandant, Don Manuel Rodríguez, was ready. Captain Shaler's mate, and co-owner of the brig, Richard Cleveland, recalled the comic opera that followed:

> *The commandant made his appearance on the shore with an escort of twelve dragoons, and, hailing the brig, requested that a boat might be sent for him. This being done he crowded his whole retinue into the boat, and on reaching the brig waited until they had climbed over the side and arranged themselves in two rows, with swords drawn and hats in hand, when he followed, and passed between them to the cabin.*

In Shaler's cabin, Rodríguez granted the captain's request for permission to come ashore and buy provisions. The commandant then departed, leaving several guards on board to watch the crew and prevent smuggling. But the sergeant of the guard quietly informed Shaler of the *Alexander* episode and the 491 confiscated pelts, which now, presumably, resided in the commandant's warehouse.

By nightfall, Shaler sent a boat crew ashore to try to acquire the otter pelts. The sailors bought a small load of black market pelts from some private parties and then arranged to send another boat for a larger quantity. The transaction turned out to be a Rodríguez sting operation. When the second boat touched shore, the commandant arrested the crew, bound them and left them under guard on the beach. The next morning, Shaler and armed sailors rowed ashore, rescued their men and returned to the *Lelia Byrd* with five Spanish soldiers as hostages.

Now it was a race to escape San Diego Bay under the guns of Fort Guijarros. From the brig, the crew could see "all bustle and animation" on shore, "both horse and foot were flocking to the fort." As the ship neared Ballast Point, Shaler forced the Spanish guards to stand in their uniforms, exposed in the bow where they could be seen by the fort's gunners. The Spanish fired anyway, with the frantic guards "imploring them to desist" and falling "with their faces to the deck, at every renewed discharge of the cannon."

For nearly an hour, the *Lelia Byrd* took cannon fire from the fort. A few shots struck the hull, and others damaged rigging and sails. A faint land breeze slowly pushed the brig close to the fort. Cleveland reported, "We now opened our fire, and, at the first broadside, [we] saw numbers, probably of

Based on a 1797 map by Juan Pantoja, this rare map was published in 1825 by order of Don Guadalupe Victoria, the first president of the Republic of Mexico. *Courtesy of Special Collections, San Diego Public Library.*

those who came to see the fun, scampering away up the hill at the back of the fort." A second Yankee broadside silenced the fort completely.

Finally clear of Fort Guijarros, Shaler put the trembling guards ashore at Point Loma and headed out to sea. So ended the colorful episode known as the Battle of San Diego Bay, the first and last sea engagement fought in San Diego.

RICHARD H. DANA DISCOVERS THE BEST HARBOR ON THE COAST

For landing and taking off hides, San Diego is decidedly the best place in California. The harbour is small and land-locked; there is no surf; the vessels lie within a cable's length of the beach, and the beach itself is

smooth, hard sand, without rocks or stones. For these reasons, it is used by all the vessels in the trade, as a depot.
—*Richard Henry Dana Jr., 1835*

Two Years Before the Mast by Richard Henry Dana Jr. is an American literary classic. The thrilling narrative of a voyage from Boston to the California coast in the 1830s was Dana's personal memoir of his time at sea—an account that prominently featured early San Diego.

Dana was a nineteen-year-old Harvard student who decided—after a bout of ill health—to escape school for a time and go to sea. Embarking from Boston harbor on the eighty-six-foot brig *Pilgrim* in August 1834, Dana sailed for the Pacific as a common seaman, determined to recover his health through hard work and see California.

Seven grueling months at sea followed before the *Pilgrim* anchored in San Diego Bay on March 14, 1835. San Diego was "a small, snug place," Dana wrote, but had "the best harbor on the coast." It was also the hub of the California hide trade—a lucrative business that lured the *Pilgrim* and other New England ships to the Pacific coast to trade for cattle hides collected from California ports.

The base of operations for the hide ships was a depot at La Playa, an area of beach just north of Ballast Point. The traders had built large barns at La Playa to warehouse the hides. Thousands of these "California bank notes" would accumulate in the hide houses before the ships left San Diego for the long return voyage to Boston.

Richard Henry Dana Jr. was a Harvard student on leave when he sailed before the mast on the hide ship *Pilgrim*. His adventures in California were recounted in his classic narrative *Two Years Before the Mast. Courtesy of Special Collections, San Diego Public Library.*

"Hide-droghing" was hard work for the sailors, but while in port, there were also treasured hours of leisure. Dana happily described his first day of liberty, a Sunday in San Diego:

> *Our crew fell in with some who belonged to the other vessels, and sailor-like, steered for the first grog-shop. This was a small mud building, of only one room, in which were liquors, dry and West India goods, shoes, bread, fruits, and everything which is vendible in California. It was kept by a Yankee, a one-eyed man, who belonged formerly to Fall River* [Massachusetts], *came out to the Pacific in a whale-ship, left her at the Sandwich Islands* [Hawaii], *and came to California and set up a "Pulperia."*

After the grogshop, Dana and a shipmate named Simpson decided to explore the countryside on two horses rented for the sum of one dollar per day:

> *The first place we went to was the old ruinous presidio, which stands on a rising ground near the village, which it overlooks. It is built in the form of an open square, like all the other presidios, and was in a most ruinous state, with the exception of one side, in which the commandant lived with his family. There were only two guns, one of which was spiked, and the other had no carriage. Twelve, half clothed, and half starved looking fellows, composed the garrison; and they, it was said, had not a musket a piece.*

Seaman Richard Dana found the Mission San Diego de Alcalá "decidedly striking in its appearance." This image, "sketched by Col. [Cave J.] Couts," is actually based on the work of artist H.M.T. Powell, who drew and sold drawings of San Diego in 1850. *Courtesy of Special Collections, San Diego Public Library.*

A Frontier Port

The small town of San Diego lay just below the presidio. It was a motley settlement of "about forty dark brown looking huts, or houses," less than half the size of Monterey or Santa Barbara.

More satisfying to Dana was the mission of San Diego de Alcalá, which the sailors found "after a pleasant ride of a couple of miles." The mission complex was built of mud bricks, but "there was something decidedly striking in its appearance." Dana was particularly impressed by the church tower with its five belfries, each with "a large bell, and immense rusty iron crosses at the tops."

At the mission, Dana and Simpson were offered wine and a meal of "baked meats, frijoles stewed with peppers and onions, boiled eggs, and California flour baked into a kind of macaroni." For sailors who had just spent seven months eating boiled meat and hard tack, "it was regal banquet."

Leaving the mission, the sailors returned to town at a full gallop. ("California horses have no medium gait," Dana discovered.)

> Coming into the village, we found things looking very lively. The Indians, who always have a holy day on Sunday, were engaged at playing a kind of running game of ball; on a level piece of ground…men, boys and girls— were chasing the ball, and throwing it with all their might…Several blue jackets were reeling about among the houses, which showed the pulperias had been well patronized.

Two weeks later, the *Pilgrim* left San Diego to collect hides at other California ports. When the ship returned in May, Dana stayed behind and spent the summer unloading ships, curing hides and storing them in the barns at "Hide Park." Many more days were spent exploring the country, meeting the people and learning their customs.

He would return Boston on another ship, the *Alert*, finally arriving in Boston in September 1836. His vigor restored, Dana returned to Harvard for his degree and began a long professional career in law, with expertise in maritime issues.

Two Years Before the Mast was written, Dana said, "to present the life of a common sailor at sea as it really is." A national bestseller when it was published in 1840, the book has never been out of print and remains today a splendid, firsthand account of life in early California.

WAR COMES TO THE PUEBLO

July 29—8 to meridian. At 10:30 hauled up courses, standing in for harbor of San Diego. At 11:30 came in to 9½ fathoms; hoisted out boats...At 3:40 the launch and Alligator *under command of Lieutenant Rowan, and the Marine Guard under Lieutenant Maddox, left the ship to take possession of the town of San Diego.*
—*log of the USS* Cyane

On Wednesday morning, July 29, 1846, a navy sloop of war, the USS *Cyane*, sailed into San Diego Bay and dropped anchor at La Playa. Four hours later, sailors and marines from the ship raised the first American flag over the small Mexican pueblo.

The U.S.-Mexican War was barely three months old, but U.S. forces were already making an aggressive claim for Alta California. In early July, the navy had raised the flag in Monterey. Commodore Robert F. Stockton, commander of the Pacific Squadron, ordered Commander Samuel Francis DuPont, of the *Cyane*, to sail from Monterey and take possession of San Diego.

Carrying 160 soldiers of John C. Fremont's California Battalion, the *Cyane* entered a quiet San Diego harbor and asked the town's Mexican authorities

The USS Cyane Taking Possession of San Diego Old Town July 1846, oil painting by Carlton T. Chapman (1860–1925). *Courtesy of Maritime Museum of San Diego.*

to raise the American flag. When they refused, DuPont directed his executive officer, Lieutenant Stephen Rowan, to take the town.

"Landing with the Marine guard and a few sailors, I marched up to the town a few miles away," Rowan later wrote, "and, having read the proclamation, hoisted the flag without opposition." That evening, Major Fremont began taking his soldiers ashore to secure San Diego.

Despite the initial reluctance over the change in flags, San Diegans greeted the American troops warmly. Commander DuPont was impressed by the town's "orderly character and friendliness" to the American cause. "We have found it very pleasant," DuPont wrote in a letter to his wife. "These people are all intelligent, and make it a much more agreeable place than Monterey."

DuPont was particularly impressed with the town's leading citizen, Don Juan Bandini. Long a fixture in California's Mexican government, Bandini was betting early on that the Yankees would soon win all of California. Bandini opened his fine house (preserved today in Old Town State Park) to the Americans and hosted "music and dancing every night."

Commander DuPont thoroughly enjoyed his stay in San Diego. Donning a Panama hat and a blouse over his uniform coat, he toured the countryside on a hired horse. On one occasion, he headed for the Mission San Diego de Alcalá, six miles beyond the town. "The buildings were good, picturesquely situated, with a church. But now all is in a mournful state of decay. Miserable naked Indians were around the piazza. We were received most hospitably by the old

Commander Samuel Francis DuPont, of the navy sloop of war the USS *Cyane*, took possession of the Mexican pueblo San Diego on July 29, 1846. *Courtesy of Special Collections, San Diego Public Library.*

padre, a Franciscan, a perfect Friar Tuck, who was what sailors term 'two sheets in the wind.'"

DuPont's tour would last only a week before orders came to depart for San Pedro. While the *Cyane* sailed north, Major Fremont took his California battalion overland to Los Angeles and quickly took control of the town. The initial conquests were easy—keeping them proved to be another matter. The Californios recaptured Los Angeles in October and then headed south to take back San Diego. Frightened citizens abandoned the pueblo and took refuge in the harbor on an anchored whaling ship, the *Stonington*. The refugees soon saw the Mexican flag reappear over the town plaza.

Rescuers arrived from San Pedro in mid-October and assembled to retake the town. An adventuresome young New Yorker, Albert B. Smith, went ashore from the *Stonington*, raced to Presidio Hill and spiked several Mexican cannons.

The Californios then abandoned the town without a fight, but not before hauling down their own flag to save it from the Americans. Albert Smith continued his heroics by shimmying up the flag pole to reattach the American flag. A few Californios reportedly shot at Smith, who waved his hat in defiance.

More reinforcements arrived in early November, when Commodore Stockton entered the port aboard his ship *Congress*. His men rebuilt a crude Mexican stronghold on the heights of Presidio Hill. Fort Stockton consisted of several cannons surrounded by a moat backed by dirt-filled whale oil barrels from the *Stonington*.

Meanwhile, marching from the east, the Army of the West under General Stephen Watts Kearny was nearing San Diego. On December 6, Kearny's one hundred dragoons stumbled into the Californio cavalrymen of Andrés Pico. The Battle of San Pasqual was a disastrous rout, with Kearny losing twenty-two dead. Three couriers, including the famed frontiersman Kit Carson, crawled through the Californio lines to get help from San Diego.

Kearny's little army would stagger into San Diego on December 12. After recovering for two weeks, the soldiers headed north to Los Angeles. Shortly before their departure, the *Cyane* returned to San Diego. Much of the sloop's crew was assigned to the force marching north, leaving too few sailors to leave port. DuPont's men busied themselves by refitting the *Stonington*—"a worthless old tub"—for future service.

The war in California ended with two skirmishes fought near San Gabriel on January 8–9, 1847. A peace treaty was signed four days later by John C. Fremont and Andrés Pico.

San Diego's leading citizen, Don Juan Bandini, and his daughter Ysidora, photographed about 1856. "These people are all intelligent," wrote Commander DuPont, "and make it a much more agreeable place than Monterey." *Courtesy of Special Collections, San Diego Public Library.*

The *Cyane* remained in San Diego for the remainder of the month. It was a festive time. The town had transitioned smoothly to American authority, and the populace was happy. DuPont would celebrate by hosting San Diegans aboard his ship: "I have invited all the Bandinis, and all of society, for they are all intermarried, to spend Saturday night aboard the *Cyane*. I believe the circle of San Diego consists of eight ladies, old and young. They were so kind to us last summer when we first took possession here, and since our arrival, that I have long wanted to pay them some civility."

The *Cyane*'s departure on January 31 closed a remarkable six-month period in San Diego history. The town's vital role as a naval port had been crucial to the success of the American victory over Mexico in California. In 1852, President Millard Fillmore would approve the acquisition of land along Point Loma as a federal reserve for harbor defenses—formally establishing a relationship that had begun with the flag raising of July 1846.

THE DAVIS FOLLY

Of the new town of San Diego, now the city of San Diego, I can say that I was its founder.
—*William Heath Davis, interview with* San Diego Sun, *December 1887*

Often forgotten in San Diego history is the pioneer some historians regard as the true founder of the city of San Diego. William Heath Davis certainly believed

William Heath Davis as he would have appeared when he started "New Town." *From Davis,* Seventy-five Years in California *(San Francisco: John Howell, 1929).*

he deserved credit for his attempt of 1850—an effort that failed but paved the way for a later city builder named Alonzo E. Horton.

Davis, the son of a Boston trader, was born in Hawaii in 1822. At age sixteen, he settled in California to learn business with his uncle. In San Francisco, he grew wealthy as a successful merchant and ship owner. Davis was a frequent visitor to the Mexican pueblo of San Diego, where, in 1847, he married into the prominent Californio family of Estudillo. His wife, María de Jesus, was the niece of José Antonio Estudillo, alcalde of San Diego (whose home, La Casa de Estudillo, is preserved today in Old Town).

During a visit to San Diego in February 1850, the chief surveyor for the U.S. Boundary Commission, Andrew Belcher Gray, introduced himself to Davis. Gray pointed out to Davis what many San Diegans thought was obvious—the future of the town lay near the port, not inland at Old Town below Presidio Hill. The surveyor recognized Davis as a man with capital and suggested a partnership to establish a new town site. The two men brought in San Diegans José Antonio Aguirre, Miguel de Pedrorena and William C. Ferrell and the local U.S. Army quartermaster, Lieutenant Thomas D. Johns, as associates in their city building scheme.

Twenty-eight-year-old William Heath Davis, "being flush, and having a large income," was the principal investor in the plan and supervised the first purchase of pueblo land: $2,304 for 160 acres bounded by the waterfront and today's Front Street and Broadway. Davis invested $60,000 for construction of a wharf and warehouse to attract ships to the new site. Land donated to the military for an army barracks completed the nucleus of "New Town" San Diego.

Davis's "New Town" or "New San Diego" showed promise. A small community grew around the plaza of Pantoja Park, at Fourth (G Street) and India. The nearby San Diego Barracks gave the town a steady population of soldiers, who happily patronized the billiard room and saloon at Davis's new hotel, the Pantoja House. The arrival of newspaper publisher John Judson Ames was a coup for Davis; Ames's *Herald*, San Diego's first newspaper, began from an office above a store in New Town in May 1851.

While New Town seemed ideally situated at the port, the location had flaws. Lack of fresh water was a major problem. With no local streams or artesian wells, the soldiers at the barracks were forced to make daily "water-train" excursions to the San Diego River, miles away near Old Town. Davis spent considerable money boring wells before good water was found.

What New Town needed most was settlers and homes. Davis ordered thousands of feet of lumber, redwood pilings, bricks, girders—all the materials necessary to construct a town. Davis even ordered a shipment of prefabricated frame houses from Portland, Maine. (San Diego's oldest surviving wooden building—intended as Davis's own home, though he never lived there—was such a house, shipped around the Horn from the East Coast.)

Andrew Gray, now on the East Coast, encouraged Davis. "Ten years—and you will still be young—and will be surrounded by a delightful population," Gray wrote. He also advised the young city builder, "Attach to your wharf—where it passes over the sand spit—a bathing house for ladies and gentlemen…this would be a great attraction and profitable also."

But most San Diegans were slow to embrace the new site. The county seat and center of the population was still Old Town, where suspicious residents showed no interest in supporting a rival town. San Francisco's leading newspaper, *Alta California*, predicted failure for the Davis venture, declaring in September 1851, "The establishment of the new town at the head of the bay was certainly a most disastrous speculation, an immense amount having been sunk in the operation."

To pay for his speculation, Davis increasingly drew on his San Francisco investments. Debts piled up. In July 1850—only months after his initial purchase of San Diego land—Davis expressed his frustration to a friend:

> *All the funds that I have drawn from the store and other sources have been eaten up in the expenses of the town…without me God only know what they would do here—it has taken an enormous sum to meet all their demands. We meet with much opposition from the inhabitants of the old town and beach—they make every effort in the world to crush us…I am on my back and unwell.*

At its peak, New Town held perhaps two hundred residents. Most drifted to Old Town in 1851–52. When Ames moved his *Herald* there in 1853, local businesses followed. Davis gave up also and returned to San Francisco, still hopeful that his venture would eventually succeed.

John Russell Bartlett, a U.S. surveyor like Andrew Gray, summarized the experiment that would be called Davis's Folly in February 1852:

> *A large and fine wharf was built here at great expense; but there is no business to bring vessels here, except an occasional one with government stores. There is no water nearer than the San Diego River, three miles distant…wood has to be brought some eight or ten miles; nor is there any arable land within four miles. Without wood, water, or arable land this place can never rise to importance.*

Ultimately, Bartlett would be proved wrong. Fifteen years later, a new city builder, Alonzo Horton, arrived from San Francisco. The businessman gazed at the site of New Town and called it "Heaven on Earth…the best spot for building a city I ever saw." Horton successfully renewed the project that failed for Davis and began the city we know today.

Ironically, Horton and his wife Sarah lived for a time in the William Heath Davis House at Market and State Streets. San Diego's oldest frame house still stands today, preserved by the Gaslamp Quarter Historical Foundation, at its current location, 410 Island Avenue.

A Library for San Diego

> *The Free Public Library…this literary resort is fast becoming a most popular place for lovers of reading, and those who wish to spend a quiet afternoon with their favorite author…The public appreciate the commodious, well ventilated apartments now occupied by the institution, and its patronage is increasing accordingly.*
> —San Diego Union, *June 28, 1889*

San Diego's "literary resort," the public library, was founded on May 19, 1882. After years of stalled efforts, which included a short-lived library started by Alonzo Horton and a casually run Free Reading Room Association, five publicly elected library trustees met to organize the city's first municipal library.

With two weeks of work, the trustees secured a suite of five rent-free rooms for the library on the second floor of the Commercial Bank on Fifth

San Diego's first public library was at the Commercial Bank on Fifth and G Streets, where it shared a floor with a dentist. *Courtesy of Special Collections, San Diego Public Library.*

and G Streets, where it shared space with a dentist, Daniel Cave. The library opened on July 15 as a reading room only; book-borrowing privileges were not considered.

The collection was started with books inherited from the failed Free Reading Room Association, augmented by new gifts and donated furniture. Magazine and newspaper subscriptions composed much of the new collection. The library trustees met regularly in the parlor of the bank building—soon known as the Consolidated National Bank—to vote on new book purchases and subscriptions.

Most purchased books were ordered from Dodge and Burbeck, a bookstore on Fifth and D Streets. These included popular modern titles such as Bullfinch's *Age of Fable*, Mark Twain's *Innocents Abroad* and Carlyle's *French Revolution*. One donation brought a large set of classical works from Homer, Sophocles, Euripides and Thucydides. The small but diverse reference collection included encyclopedias, biographies, government reports, law books and books written in Latin, Greek, French and German.

The trustees apparently felt there was no need for a trained professional to oversee the library. The collection was supervised by a caretaker, Archibald Hooker, who was also the janitor.

Janitor-librarian Hooker was authorized to "let out books" beginning in June 1883, but the circulation rules were strict. Borrowers were required to "furnish good security for their return," or leave a deposit for the full price of the book. The rules were later clarified to specify that "all property owners" could check out books by applying for a library card. All other borrowers needed their library card applications co-signed by a city resident, presumably a property owner.

Augustus Wooster, a local attorney, was hired as "librarian" in 1884 with a monthly salary of ten dollars. He was replaced in September 1887 by Lulu Younkin, a former teacher and graduate of the University of Iowa. Hired at seventy-five dollars per month, Miss Younkin was asked to "take charge of the library and to index the books."

Miss Younkin eagerly arranged the book collection by the Dewey decimal system and produced a 212-page catalogue, which itemized the seven-thousand-volume collection. A chapter on Rules and Regulations stated that books could be checked out for two weeks by borrowers twelve years of age or older. Overdue fines were five cents a day, but severely late books could be "sent for" with a surcharge of twenty-five cents.

As customary for the day, the library shelves were closed to the public. Books needed to be requested from the librarian, and no one was admitted behind a rope placed in front of the shelves. "Free access to the books was the source of much annoyance to the librarian and loss to the library," Miss Younkin explained.

But the "closed stacks" policy also annoyed the library trustees, who preferred "giving the public all the privileges possible, even at the expense of an occasional loss to the library." After many complaints from library users, they ordered Miss Younkin to remove her rope and permit free access to the shelves. The trustees appeased the librarian by allowing her to mark all the non-circulating magazines with the words: "Stolen from the public library."

A bank renovation came in 1889, and the library moved upstairs after two new floors had been added to the building. The fourth floor was leased for $150 per month. San Diego's *Golden Era* magazine approved of the new quarters: "The main room is 50 x 90 feet, with twenty-six windows, thereby insuring an abundance of light by day, while by night a multitude of electric jets illumine the room."

The renovated library featured two reading rooms, one for each sex. Althea Warren, the city librarian for San Diego's later Carnegie Library, recalled: "Sex determined whether you turned right or left on climbing the stairs to the second floor." The rooms were identical; "the only way to tell them apart was that the women's reading room held a potted palm."

San Diego librarian Lulu Younkin was a former schoolteacher from Iowa. *Courtesy of Special Collections, San Diego Public Library.*

The library was open daily from 9:00 a.m. until 9:00 p.m., with one-hour lunch and dinner breaks for Miss Younkin and her two assistants. Sunday hours were 1:00 to 4:00 p.m.

By the late 1880s, the public library had become a major downtown success story. The two reading rooms were usually crowded, particularly in the evening hours. Book circulation figures were remarkable: 5,855 volumes circulated in October 1889. Annual circulation neared 70,000.

The local newspapers were consistent boosters of the library. The *Union* declared that the San Diego Public Library, "in proportion to its size," supplied more reading than any other library in California. "This being the fact," the newspaper asked, "will not every citizen do all in his power to promote its development?"

But financial support from the city government was minimal and rarely enough to grow the collection or even replace worn-out books. Rising utility bills forced the library to turn down lights. The library appealed to the Consolidated Bank for lower rent, but the bank refused.

As a cost-saving measure, the library signed a five-year lease in April 1993 for second-floor rooms in the St. James Hotel near the corner of Seventh and F Streets. Only six weeks later, the library reopened. "The arrangement of the large, airy rooms has been completed in an excellent manner," the *Union* reported. "The public will doubtless be well satisfied with the change."

The St. James would be the home of the public library for the next five years. After another location change, to the top floor of the Keating Building at Fifth and F Streets, a spirited public campaign would raise funds for the city's first library building. With a $60,000 donation from Andrew Carnegie, the city would build a new library at Eighth and E Streets, finished in 1902.

BUILDING A CITY

THE GREAT BOOM OF THE EIGHTIES

It was plain that they were in fact buying comfort, immunity from snow and slush, from piercing winds and sleet-clad streets, from sultry days and sleepless nights, from thunderstorms, cyclones, malaria, mosquitoes and bedbugs. All of which, in plain language, means that they were buying climate.
—*Theodore S. Van Dyke, in* Millionaires of a Day, *1890*

"Bay'n climate," some people called it. The irresistible twin lure of a beautiful harbor and an equitable climate drew tens of thousands to San Diego between 1885 and 1887—a period of furious growth called the "boom of the eighties." Within an eighteen-month period, San Diego's population exploded from about five thousand to an estimated forty thousand people.

The great boom began with the railroads. San Diegans had always been desperate for a rail connection to the East, which they believed would end geographic isolation and bring people and prosperity. Railroad schemes and projects came and went. Finally, in 1885, the transcontinental railroad reached San Diego. A train from the California Southern, a subsidiary of Santa Fe, pulled into town on November 21, and the boom was on.

A rate war between Santa Fe and its chief competitor, the Southern Pacific, spurred passenger traffic. A $125 ticket from Missouri to Southern California dropped to $100 and then started to plunge. By March 1887,

Boomtown San Diego about 1887. This image shows Fifth Street (today's Fifth Avenue) looking north from H Street (Market). *Courtesy of Special Collections, San Diego Public Library.*

the rate had fallen to $12, and for a time, $1 bought a ticket from St. Louis to San Diego.

As the rail passengers flooded into town, the hotels and rooming houses filled, leading the *San Diego Union* to warn: "An unwary stranger who neglects to engage a room immediately on his arrival here is often compelled to sit in a chair through the night for want of a bed."

Wild real estate speculation was led by land syndicates that bought large tracts of old Mexican ranchos and then subdivided the land for new town sites. The syndicates sold lots to eager investors, lured to noisy auctions by free transportation, barbeques and band music. Some twenty new towns emerged in San Diego County, including Oceanside, Escondido, San Marcos, Ramona, El Cajon, Santee, Lakeside, Otay and Chula Vista.

The most successful town project was Coronado, the brush-covered peninsula in San Diego Bay that promoter Elisha S. Babcock turned into a seaside resort with his million-dollar Hotel del Coronado. The Babcock syndicate bought seven thousand acres of Coronado land for $110,000 and then earned $2 million selling individual lots at auction.

The most visible results of the boom were in the city of San Diego, which quickly transformed itself with new construction and civic institutions. Author and promoter Theodore Van Dyke observed at the height of the boom:

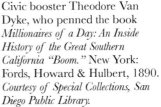

Civic booster Theodore Van Dyke, who penned the book *Millionaires of a Day: An Inside History of the Great Southern California "Boom."* New York: Fords, Howard & Hulbert, 1890. *Courtesy of Special Collections, San Diego Public Library.*

New stores, hotels, and dwellings are arising on every hand from the center to the farthest outskirts in more bewildering numbers than before, and people are pouring in at double the rate they did but six months ago. It is impossible to keep track of its progress. No one seems any longer to know or care who is putting up the big buildings, and it is becoming difficult to find a familiar face in the crowd or at the hotels.

New urban infrastructure accompanied the building boom. Streets were graded and sidewalks laid. A bond issue of $400,000 paid for thirty-eight miles of sewer pipes in downtown—a project that took only one year to complete. Public transportation came with the horse-drawn cars of the San Diego Street Railway. Arc lamps mounted on 110-foot masts illuminated the city, and the San Diego Telephone Company offered service to 284 subscribers.

The water supply, however, was a problem. The city struggled to find adequate supplies from wells until the San Diego Flume Company finished a thirty-five-mile wooden aqueduct that carried water from the Cuyamacas to city pipes. Fast-growing National City dealt with its water issue by building the Sweetwater Dam and reservoir.

Churches, the YMCA and the Woman's Christian Temperance Union addressed the spiritual needs of boomtown San Diego—quite a task considering the scores of saloons and gambling halls emerging between H Street (Market) and the bay. Book readers found the public library, which was housed on the second floor of the Commercial Bank building at Fifth and G Streets. The city directory noted the library's "well-filled rooms are ample evidence of the culture and intelligence of the people of the City."

For all of San Diego's progress, there was little doubt that real estate speculation, which reached a frenzied height in late 1887, was a looming disaster. Local historian Walter Gifford Smith wrote:

> *Land advanced daily in selling price and fortunes were made on margins. A $5000 sale was quickly followed by a $10,000 transfer of the same property, and in three months a price of $50,000 was reached. Excitement became a kind of lunacy, and business men persuaded themselves that San Diego would soon cover an area which, soberly measured, was seen to be larger than that of London.*

In the spring of 1888, the bubble burst. Tightening credit slowed property sales, and the speculators disappeared. When word got out that the Santa Fe Railroad was moving its offices north—meaning San Diego would no longer be the western terminus of the railroad—an estimated ten thousand "boomers" left town. Houses stood vacant, and building projects stopped.

But the boom had permanently changed San Diego. Beautiful buildings filled the Gaslamp Quarter—structures that survive today. A new city charter established a modern local government. Professional fire and police departments were started. A small town had become a city.

THE TELEPHONE COMES TO SAN DIEGO

Lieutenant Philip Reade, Officer in Charge, Signal Service, U.S.A. at San Diego, returned to the city yesterday, after a brief trip to San Francisco, bringing with him a telephone…On his way down he stopped at Los Angeles, where he gave an experimental exhibition of the wonderful talking instrument. As soon as he can get the telephone set up here he will give us all an opportunity to hold conversation over the wire, and see (or rather, hear) for ourselves what it will do.
—San Diego Union, *November 29, 1877*

Less than two years after Alexander Graham Bell's successful invention of the telephone, the mysterious hand gadget appeared in San Diego. A U.S. weather officer, Lieutenant Philip Reade, had discovered the telephone on a business trip to San Francisco, where he met Gardiner Hubbard, founder of the recently organized Bell Telephone Company and father-in-law of the inventor. Eager to promote business in California, Hubbard loaned Reade three telephone sets, which the lieutenant brought back to San Diego.

Reade took the telephones to J.W. Thompson, the manager of the local Western Union telegraph office. The men ran wires from the office to their homes and began experimenting. "I shall never forget the sensation I experienced the first time I used the telephone," Thompson recalled in his memoirs. "The voice came faint yet clear, seemed as if the voice was down in a deep well and it was almost the limit of hearing."

On December 5, 1877, Reade and Thompson offered the first public demonstration of the telephone in San Diego. Sergeant Samuel Patton, a telegraph operator for the U.S. Signal Service, took a telephone east out of town and connected it to a telegraph line. "A lively and animated conversation" followed, reported the *Union*, including a "rattling" rendition of "Yankee Doodle" whistled over the wires by Sergeant Patton eighteen miles away.

The men repeated the experiment the next day by connecting the line from Campo, about forty miles east. "Tunes were whistled, songs were sung, and various sounds transmitted with astonishing accuracy," reported the newspaper. An exhibition and lecture held at Horton Hall on December 31 thrilled a large audience, which took turns using the device to talk to the Signal Service office a few blocks away, an "amusing practical exposition of telephony."

San Diego's first telephone was a wooden, bell-shaped instrument used for both transmission and reception. The user put the bell to the mouth to speak and then to the ear to hear the reply. Wires ran from the bell to batteries and then to the transmission line—usually telegraph wire in the early years. Most telephone users confirmed Thompson's impression of audio quality as "faint yet clear."

Lieutenant Reade continued to test his telephone in the first few months of 1878, gradually increasing the distances used. One "triumphal test" connected San Diego to Yuma, Arizona. The "200 mile" distance was "the greatest yet attained with the hand telephone," claimed the *Union*.

Three years would pass before the telephone in San Diego made its next evolutionary step: a "telephone exchange" that linked service to subscribers

San Diego Telephone Exchange,

CENTRAL OFFICE, COR. SIXTH AND G STREETS.

(With the Western Union Telegraph, Wells, Fargo & Co's Express, and General Stage Offices.)

LIST OF SUBSCRIBERS.

NAMES.	No.	LOCATION.	NAMES.	No.	LOCATION.
Allison Brothers.	142	Market.	Kimball, F. A.	45	National City
" "	145	Slaugh. House.	Leach & Parker	18	Office.
California Southern R. R.	42	General Office.	Luce, M. A.	20	Office.
" " "	43	National City.	Pacific Coast S. S. Co.	82	Office.
Campo	25		" " " "	83	End of Wharf.
Chase, Chas. A.	9	Drug Store.	Reed, D. C.	144	Residence.
Clark & Russell	22	Stable.	Remondino, Dr. P. C.	122	Residence.
Consolidated Bank	17		Russ & Company.	5	Lumber Yard.
Court House	11		" "	44	National City.
Fairchild, J. A.	32	Office.	San Diego Flour Mills	73	
" "	33	Residence.	Steiner, Klauber & Co.	72	
Francisco, Silliman & Co.	15		Stockton, Dr. T. C.	123	Residence.
Gas Works.	16		" " " "	126	Office.
Hamilton & Co	24		Stewart, W. W.	21	Warehouse.
Hinton & Gordon	102	Livery Stable.	Sun Office	6	
Hinton, J. B.	103	Residence.	Thompson, J. W.	13	Residence.
Horton, A. E.	143	Residence.	Union Office	2	
Horton House	19		Wentscher, A.	12	Office.
Infirmary	124		" "	13	Warehouse.
			" "	23	Residence.

NOTICE.

To facilitate rapid switching, each subscriber's wire will be designated by a number placed opposite his name on the right hand. Subscribers having more than one telephone station on the same wire, are designated by a small figure at the right of their telephone number, which figure is also the number of bells for that station. Call the Central Office, and give the number of the wire instead of the name of the person you wish to converse with. When switch is made ring again for the number wanted. Do not place the mouth too near the transmitter when talking. Report all interruptions to the Central Office.

Always hang the Telephone on the hook when not in use.

J. W. THOMPSON, Manager.

San Diego's first telephone directory was a five- by seven-inch manila card provided to subscribers in July 1881. *Courtesy of Special Collections, San Diego Public Library.*

in the city. In June 1881, J.W. Thompson opened the San Diego Telephone Exchange alongside the office of Western Union at the corner of Sixth and G Streets. For a town of about 2,600 people, the exchange was a remarkable achievement and heralded by the *Union* as "one of the significant 'signs of the times' that marks the progress of the city."

The first telephone directory appeared in July: a half-sheet card listing thirty-one customers. The subscribers paid a monthly rate of four dollars after a twenty-dollar installation fee for each telephone (longer-distance runs, such as the telephone line to National City, cost considerably more). The high cost of the service ensured that businesses took all but eight of the phone lines. Personal ownership of phones was rare; city founder Alonzo Horton had a private phone, and so did the town's most successful physician, P.C. Remondino.

Communities outside the city of San Diego soon clamored for phone service. After Thompson installed a line linking the mining towns of Julian and Banner, the townspeople started a fundraising drive to construct their own line to San Diego. Wealthy rancher George Cowles led the effort to string phone lines to El Cajon—"a nice thing to have plenty of 'tin' and know how to use it," remarked a reporter.

The army telegraph line to Campo was suggested by the *Union* as a means of linking the "settlers" of the east county. "If the residents of Jamul, of Cottonwood and Potrero would club together and have one telephone placed at a convenient place at each of the above localities the expense would be very light."

Telephone connections to the world outside of San Diego County remained experimental. On March 28, 1882, the *Los Angeles Times* reported a successful trial between San Diego and Los Angeles using a telegraph line—"not first-class, having been in use twelve years." The *Times* concluded that with proper wire the telephone was "a reliable message bearer for one hundred miles and better."

As San Diego grew in the mid-1880s, seemingly every new phone installation was announced in the newspapers. By 1885, the San Diego Telephone Company, now in larger quarters at 813 Fifth, controlled sixty-five telephones, with connections ably managed by the first female phone operator, Mrs. W.F. McGrath. With the boom of the eighties and a population nearing thirty thousand in 1887, the number of telephones grew to nearly three hundred.

In December 1890, the San Diego Telephone Company was bought by the Sunset Telephone and Telegraph Company, a rapidly growing corporation based in San Francisco. J.W. Thompson continued as manager until 1895. Two years later, the company completed a long-distance line to Santa Ana, connecting San Diego County for the first time to the cities and towns of California.

"Sanitary engineer" Colonel George E. Waring Jr. designed San Diego's first sewer system. *Library of Congress.*

THE SEWERING OF THE CITY

Mr. Kitterman has taken the precaution to construct a sewer from his restaurant to the bay. Patrons of the establishment declare that it is one of the nicest places in town since the completion of the improvement, and say that the immunity from flies is remarkable.
—San Diego Union, *September 1, 1872*

Fifth Street restaurant owner Alex Kitterman knew the value of a good sewer. Other businessmen and residents also recognized that proper disposal of wastewater had become essential in downtown San Diego. But with no government oversight, privately built sewers, privies and cesspools multiplied in the 1870s—some emptying their odiferous loads on the beaches of San Diego Bay and others simply spilling into city streets.

San Diegans coped with the haphazard sewers until the mid-1880s, when the City Board of Trustees tried to address complaints of "vile exhalations and odors" with an ordinance mandating official approval of all private sewer plans. The new law specified the proper construction materials for pipe and declared that the sewers "must be extended at least to medium low tide water in the Bay of San Diego."

But with a booming population—thousands of people were arriving monthly by railroad or steamship—it was clear that a municipal system was necessary. Public health demanded it. Cities in the East had suffered from frightful outbreaks of cholera and typhoid fever, attributed to pollution from raw sewage.

"We want the very best system of sewerage that the most competent sanitary engineering skill can give us," the *San Diego Union* editorialized on November 28, 1885. The newspaper insisted that the city trustees "communicate immediately" with Colonel George E. Waring Jr. of Rhode Island, "the most eminent sanitary engineer in the country."

Waring had worked on the construction of New York's Central Park in 1857. After serving the Union cause in the Civil War, he became a noted municipal engineer and was best known for his construction of a sewage system for Memphis, Tennessee. In the 1870s, devastating epidemics of cholera and yellow fever in Memphis had killed thousands of people. Once the "Waring System" was in place, the epidemics ended.

San Diego's city trustees contacted Colonel Waring and then studied his written reply in June 1886. The engineer offered to provide plans and complete specifications for a fee of $1,000. The trustees voted unanimously to adopt Waring's proposal.

The plan for the new city sewer system. *From Waring*, Sewerage and Land Drainage *(New York: D. Van Nostrand Company, 1889)*.

Six months later, the colonel's detailed strategy for "sewering the city" arrived in San Diego. The plan specified forty total miles of sewer lines running down the center of the city streets with smaller, lateral pipes entering the system from all buildings. The main lines would be vitrified clay pipe, twenty-four inches in diameter; smaller pipes narrowed to eight inches. The sewage was forced through the pipes by large water tanks that discharged twice a day to flush the untreated sewage westward for an unceremonious ocean burial.

The proposed dumping of sewage into San Diego Bay elicited minor controversy. The *Union* published an anonymous letter to the editor, which complained that "to empty the city sewage into the bay anywhere this side of Ballast Point would be a crime" and would inevitably "befoul the margin of the whole bay." Colonel Waring scoffed at the concern, replying that the sewage was "little worse than dirty water." Besides, "fish and animalculae" would consume much of the wastewater.

Building a City

To pay for their new sewers, the Board of Trustees proposed—and voters approved—a $400,000 bond measure. Work began on July 26, 1887. Progress was erratic at first. Supplies of materials arrived slowly, and there was difficulty in getting laborers. All work stopped in early August when the ditch diggers went on strike, protesting a contractor's cut in wages from $2.25 a day to $2.00. The work resumed with a change in contractor.

The eight-foot-deep trenches were dug mostly done by hand, aided by the liberal use of dynamite. "The heavy reports heard last night were caused by blasting that was being done on the Fourth-street sewer," the *Union* reported. "Owing to the large amount of travel on that street in the daytime, it is safe to blast only at night."

Night construction could be hazardous for people walking after dark. The workers hung lanterns over trench sites, but the lights were often poorly placed. "Much complaint is being made by citizens regarding the placing of signal lights," a newspaper warned. "Several narrow escapes of citizens falling into the sewer are reported."

Digging the sewer trenches meant tearing up a recently built streetcar line on Fourth Street. It also postponed plans to grade the city's dirt streets and

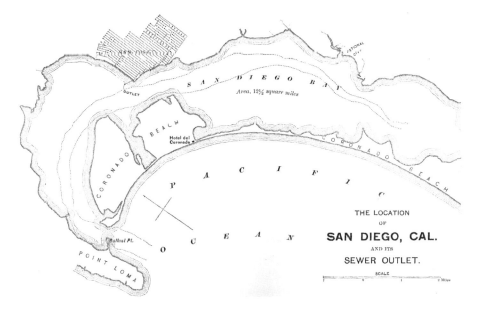

The city sewer system emptied into San Diego Bay. Planners believed outgoing tides would carry waste beyond Point Loma and out to sea. *From Waring,* Sewerage and Land Drainage *(New York: D. Van Nostrand Company, 1889).*

pave them with asphalt. "Nothing can be done," mourned the *Union*, "until the sewers, both main and lateral, have been completed."

Fitfully, the construction proceeded. The sewer lines migrated downhill at a slight grade to the bayside at the foot of H Street (Market). From here a thirty-inch iron pipe carried the sewage 1,100 feet across the bay to the "grand feature" of the system: an immense sewer vat 200 feet square.

Built of creosoted lumber—until the city could afford concrete—the 1,500,000-gallon vat collected sewage until just after high tide, when an automatic gate mechanism opened and "the great pool of sewage floated out with the receding tide." Colonel Waring believed the tidal surge would carry the sewage "beyond Ballast Point and mainly beyond Point Loma, with no probability of its return."

On July 4, 1888, the city proclaimed the project completed. The *Union* heralded the system as the "most complete sewer plant that exists anywhere in the world in a city of less than 250,000 people." Twenty years later, William Smythe's *History of San Diego* would boast that the Waring System still efficiently served San Diego, "a model of engineering skill and of public spirit."

A FLOATING FOREST TO BUILD A CITY

Prolonged blasts from nearly all the steam whistles in town heralded the arrival of the big Benson log raft at noon today…during its slow passage up the bay crowds of people hastened to the water front. Before the big mass of timber had reached the wharves all the docks were lined with spectators.
—San Diego Tribune, *September 8, 1906*

San Diegans were awestruck that morning as they watched the tugboat *Dauntless* steam around Point Loma towing what appeared to be a giant whale. The "whale" was an oceangoing raft of tree-length logs—six hundred feet long—shaped like a Perfecto cigar.

It was the first "Benson raft," named for Portland lumber magnate Simon Benson, who claimed vast tracts of timber along the Columbia River and was eager to find a cheap way to ship lumber to booming Southern California. His log raft was completing a two-week journey by sea, all the way from Astoria, Oregon, to the site of a planned Benson-owned sawmill in San Diego Bay at the foot of Sigsbee Street, south of the site of today's Convention Center.

The raft was a dramatic commercial success. Benson had found a way to circumvent the high cost of shipping lumber by railroad or ocean barge.

Under tow from the tugboat *Hercules*, a giant log raft is finishing its journey to San Diego. The Coronado ferry boat *Ramona* can be seen in the upper right. *Courtesy of Maritime Museum of San Diego.*

Soon, between 2 and 6 rafts a year arrived in San Diego, enough to keep the Benson mill well supplied with raw material. In the next thirty-five years, 120 giant rafts would make the 1,100-mile journey from Oregon down the Pacific coast to San Diego, supplying lumber for almost all major local construction projects.

Benson's rafts were assembled in winter months in calm waters of the Columbia River near Clatskanie on the Oregon border. A floating derrick lifted logs into a wooden "cradle." As the cradle filled, the logs were secured in a cigar-shaped bundle by an enormous network of chains. It took several weeks to build a typical raft that measured up to one thousand feet long, fifty-five feet wide and thirty-five feet thick. Most rafts also carried deck loads of shingles, telephone poles and finished lumber.

In summer, the log rafts were towed out to sea to begin the long trip down the coast to San Diego. The rafts moved slowly—sixty miles a day was considered a fast run. Mishaps at sea were rare. Storms would sometimes claim a few logs, but the rafts stayed intact. Benson recalled: "If we struck rough weather… the steamer cast loose [and] let the raft wallow in the trough of the sea till the storm blew itself out. Then we reattached the cable to the raft and went on."

The sea-going steamers towing the rafts were larger and more powerful than harbor tugboats. One of these steamers was the famed SS *Roosevelt*, the

San Diegans stroll aboard a floating raft on Monday afternoon, August 20, 1906. *Courtesy of Special Collections, San Diego Public Library.*

134-foot ship that carried explorer Robert E. Peary toward the North Pole in 1909. After a distinguished Arctic career, the aging *Roosevelt* became a salvage vessel, then a fishing boat and finally a log-towing tug in the 1930s.

When the rafts arrived in San Diego, the huge bundles would be disassembled by crane at the mill of the Benson Lumber Company and the timbers cut into dimension lumber. A big raft provided up to six million board feet of lumber, enough "to build 460 average residences," boasted the *San Diego Union* in 1935.

Simon Benson profited from his log rafts until 1911, when he decided to sell his San Diego interests to his mill manager, O.J. Evenson, and San Diego investor Frank C. Lynch. Evenson ran the mill until his retirement in 1936. Frank Lynch took over, but as World War II approached, the era of log rafts was nearing the end.

In August 1941, Log Raft 120 caught fire off the coast near Monterey. The mystery of how a raft of wet logs could be destroyed at sea by fire was never solved. Lynch suggested wartime sabotage. He turned the wreckage over to the underwriters and then, blaming rising insurance rates, decided to terminate the Benson rafts, ending a unique chapter in San Diego history.

THE HOUSE MOVERS

Palmer & Son created some interest yesterday by driving a house through the streets, mounted on an improvised truck. In about two hours the building was hauled not less than ten blocks. Telegraph and telephone lines along the route were demoralized.
—San Diego Union, *September 23, 1885*

Rarely seen today, house moving became a common sight in San Diego once the Palmers came to town. In the late nineteenth century, moving a building often made more economic sense than razing the structure and starting over with new materials. In San Diego, the house-moving franchise of the Palmer family moved buildings around town for over half a century.

John D. Palmer came to San Diego in May 1884 with his wife, eight children and sixteen dollars in his pocket. A Civil War veteran from Ohio, Palmer ran a sawmill in his home state for fourteen years. After a flood carried away his mill, J.D. decided to start over in California. The family took a train to Los Angeles and then embarked for San Diego on the side-wheeler steamship *Orizaba*.

In San Diego, J.D. was greeted by his father, Oscar, who had come to San Diego in 1868. Oscar managed the small Palmer House hotel—an addition, really, to the much larger Horton House—at Fifth and D Streets (Broadway). Another son, Isaac L. Palmer, was a city constable. But J.D. would be the family "mover" and shaker and patriarch to a large, community-minded family.

On July 6, 1884, only weeks after Palmer's arrival in town, the *Union* noted that "the work of moving E. Stewart's tin shop commenced yesterday under the supervision of J.D. Palmer, who has constructed a new apparatus for doing the work." It took Palmer and his crew three days to move the structure up Fifth Street. Within a week, he was at work again, moving a building on Sixth Street onto the spot vacated by Stewart's hardware store. The former furniture store evidently had some size. "Nearly all the telephone wires that cross Fifth street between E and F streets will have to be cut in order to let it pass," reported the *Union*.

Palmer's "new apparatus" for moving buildings is unknown. But he undoubtedly employed techniques that had been used in America since the early century. Typically, heavy wooden beams were inserted below the structure, which was then carefully raised by screw jacks. The building would then be lowered onto a wooden carriage, which was pulled by horses or oxen and, in later years, by steam-powered tractors and eventually heavy trucks.

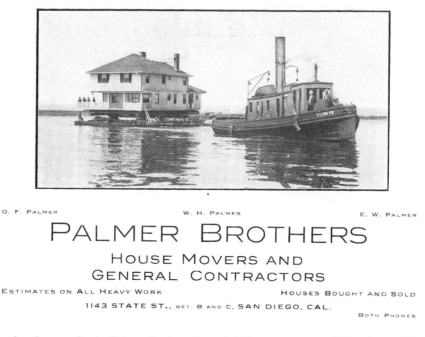

O. F. PALMER W. H. PALMER E. W. PALMER

PALMER BROTHERS
HOUSE MOVERS AND
GENERAL CONTRACTORS

ESTIMATES ON ALL HEAVY WORK HOUSES BOUGHT AND SOLD

1143 STATE ST., BET. B AND C, SAN DIEGO, CAL.

BOTH PHONES

An advertisement for the Palmer Brothers showed the house movers could handle any job, even towing a house across San Diego Bay to Coronado. *From* Souvenir, San Diego Fire Department, *December 1906.*

Palmer Brothers (John D., with sons William, Scott, Oscar and Edgar) moved anything, anywhere. On several occasions, houses were moved to the waterfront, mounted on barges and floated to Coronado Island. Russ High School was once picked up and moved two hundred feet to clear lot space in front of the school. Brick structures moved as easily as wood; the four-story Palmer House, known as "the addition," was separated and moved from the Horton House in 1905 when the larger hotel was being demolished—a job also handled by the Palmers.

But a small move proved controversial. In 1893, San Diegans decided to represent their city at the World's Columbian Exposition in Chicago by sending the fair a historic palm tree, popularly believed to have been planted by Father Junípero Serra himself. The Palmers excavated the fifty-foot tree on Taylor Street in Mission Valley, loaded it on rollers and moved it to the Santa Fe depot, where two flat cars took it to Chicago. The tree soon died there, according to a witness, Don Stewart, who called the affair "an extreme mental lapse" on the part of promoters who destroyed "one of San Diego's most historical and most interesting landmarks."

The year 1893 also brought a personal injury lawsuit that nearly destroyed Palmer Brothers. Boys playing seesaw on an eighty-seven-foot skid at a moving site on Sixteenth and I Streets knocked the timber loose, which fell and crushed the leg of seven-year-old Tommy West. The leg had to be amputated. The West family sued the Palmers to collect damages for injuries received "as a result of the defendant's carelessness in leaving heavy timbers in the street." The court awarded the family $5,000. To satisfy the claim, the Palmers were forced to sell at public auction "four draft horses, two heavy wagons, express and light wagons, harness, timbers, blocks, tackle, etc."

The next month, J.D. Palmer & Co. was declared insolvent by a Superior Court judge. But the family business would successfully reorganize and soon prosper again. William Palmer took over the firm in 1906 when John D. died suddenly from heart disease at age sixty-three. Other family members took an active part in the business, including contractor Walter J. Fulkerson, the husband of John's daughter, Maggie.

In the early 1900s the family branched out to other enterprises. Scott and his brother-in-law Walter managed the Pickwick and Savoy Theaters and brought big-time vaudeville to San Diego. William, an active sportsman, stirred interest in professional baseball in San Diego and also served two terms as a city councilman. Moving houses continued to be a Palmer family specialty, with the youngest son Edgar running the business until the late 1940s.

Law and Disorder

The Bloody River Crossing on the Colorado

When I was at San Diego, a great many complaints were made by citizens there, and persons arriving from the Gila, of a gang of lawless men who had established a ferry over the Colorado, where not only they practised the greatest extortions, but committed murders and robberies.
—letter from General Persifer Smith to Captain Irvin McDowell, May 25, 1850

The Yuma Crossing at the junction of the Colorado and Gila Rivers was once a key overland gateway to California. When the Gold Rush began in 1848, thousands of migrants hurried across the hot Sonora Desert and forded the quarter-mile-wide Colorado River at Yuma on San Diego County's eastern border.

One of the first ferry landings at Yuma was run by Dr. Able Lincoln, a physician from New York, who had recently fought in the U.S.-Mexico War. Mustered out at Mexico City in 1848, Lincoln had started for home but turned west when he heard word of the gold strikes in California. The difficult crossing of the Colorado River convinced Lincoln that a ferry business could be as valuable as gold. He built a boat and began carrying gold seekers across the river in January 1850.

Sketch of the Yuma Crossing at it appeared in 1852. *From John Russell Bartlett,* Personal Narrative of Explorations and Incidents *(New York: D. Appleton, 1854).*

The ferry was a lucrative success. Lincoln would write home to his parents in April, reporting he had ferried over twenty thousand migrants, all bound for the gold mines of California. "I have taken in over $60,000," he boasted. "My price, $1 per man, horse or mule $2, the pack $1, pack saddle 50 cents, saddle 25 cents."

Strangely, despite his profits, Lincoln did not expect to stay at the crossing longer than six months and "perhaps not more than a month." "I shall sell at the first opportunity," he wrote, adding ominously, "This is an unsafe place to live in."

Undisclosed in the letter to his family was the news that Lincoln had taken on an uninvited partner. His name was John Joel Glanton. Like Lincoln, he was a veteran of the war with Mexico. After the war, Glanton led a gang of "scalp hunters" along the borderlands, killing Apache Indians for a bounty offered by the governor of Chihuahua, Mexico: $200 per scalp for a warrior, lesser amounts for women and children. When Glanton expanded his bloody trade by killing Mexicans as well as Indians, a bounty was offered for *his* scalp. The gang headed west and arrived at the Colorado only weeks after Lincoln started his ferry.

Glanton muscled in and took over Lincoln's operation. The price of passage across the river rose to ten dollars and more, extracted at gunpoint when necessary. For the next three months, the Glanton gang robbed and terrorized migrants at the river crossing.

Competing ferries downstream from Glanton never had a chance. Persifer Smith reported:

There were two others already there—one kept by the Youmas [sic] Indians, and the other by an Irishman. This gang took the Indians' boats and cut holes in the bottoms, so as to render them unserviceable; and a few days afterwards they seized the Irishman and brought him up to their camp, where he was tied. The next morning the dead body of the Irishman, with his hands still tied, was found in the water, with a ball through his head.

Chief Caballo en Pelo of the Yumas called on Glanton to work out a deal. The Indian chief offered to give up ferrying men and baggage but would swim the animals across, "thus they would get along quietly." Glanton refused the compromise and kicked the Yumas out of camp.

Furious with the insult, the Indians vowed to kill every white man at the crossing. But before they could attack, Glanton and several of his men went to San Diego to buy supplies. The Yumas bided their time.

In San Diego, the men banked $8,000 of their profits with a local judge. They purchased their supplies and then headed back to Yuma—but not before one of Glanton's men managed to provoke a fight with a soldier in town and shoot the man dead. David Brown was quickly arrested, but with no jail in San Diego, he was placed under guard. Brown bribed the sentry and escaped to Los Angeles.

When Glanton and company returned to the ferry landing on April 21, the Indians were waiting. About noon, as many of the men slept in the midday heat, several hundred Yumas rushed the camp and clubbed to death Glanton, Lincoln and nine others. Three men chopping wood on the riverbank escaped by reaching a boat and rowing furiously downstream.

Reports of the massacre came when the three fugitives reached San Diego. Excited by the news, San Diegans held a public meeting and then petitioned the governor to send troops immediately to the Colorado "to punish a terrible murder committed on American citizens there."

Governor Peter H. Burnett ordered the commander of the California State Militia to organize an armed volunteer force and proceed to "the ferry on the Colorado, and pursue such energetic measures as may be necessary to punish the Indians, bring them to terms, and protect the emigrants on their way to California."

More than one hundred recruits from Los Angeles and San Diego headed for the river under the command of General J.C. Morehead. The Gila Expedition would be an inglorious farce. When they arrived at the river crossing four months after the massacre, the Indians had quieted down. General Morehead provoked a fight anyway. After killing about twenty

Yumas and destroying their crops, the militiamen declared victory and turned for home.

The Glanton episode did result in a permanent army post on the Colorado, established in November 1850. Soldiers from Fort Yuma would protect migrants at the river crossing for the next thirty years.

Perhaps the most interesting legacy of the Glanton gang would be the classic novel by Cormac McCarthy published in 1985. *Blood Meridian, or the Evening Redness in the West* tells the story of "the kid" and his experiences with scalp hunters led by the renegade soldier John Glanton, killed by Indians at a ferry landing on the Colorado River.

JAILBREAK

A bold, daring and successful attempt at jail breaking occurred at the county jail this morning before daylight...Four desperate characters, conspired together to break for liberty, and after careful, premeditated plans, succeeded in gaining liberty.
—Daily San Diegan, *April 23, 1888*

Since 1872, a thirty-three- by fifty-four-foot room in the rear of the county courthouse at Front and D Streets (Broadway) had served as the county jail. Iron cells filled the middle of the space, but inmates had the run of the room most of the time. At night, they slept in the cells, which were rarely locked.

It was considered a very secure prison—at least until the early morning of April 23, 1888, when four prisoners escaped before daybreak. The "daring desperadoes" were Theodore Fowler, a twenty-four-year-old ex-convict recently sentenced to ten years in San Quentin for stealing a cow; John C. Young, convicted and sentenced to San Quentin for real estate fraud; José Shock, a "Mexican Indian" and alleged horse thief; and J. Pool, alias J.S. Hair, a check forger.

For the town's three daily newspapers (serving a city population of about thirty thousand) it was the biggest news story in months. The *Daily San Diegan* described how inmates sawed off a two-inch iron bar and shattered the windowpanes "to quietly breathe the fresh air of liberty." According to the *Union*'s account, the escape had begun with an afternoon "concert" in the cellblock: "While the prisoners were singing, Fowler or Young worked at the bar, the vocalism drowning the rasping of the saw."

Photogravure of the San Diego County Courthouse on D Street (Broadway) between Front and Union. *By photographer Herve Friend. From Douglas Gunn,* Picturesque San Diego *(Chicago: 1887).*

That night, the prisoners dropped quietly from the debarred window on the west side of the courthouse and then scaled a high plank fence. Fresh horse hooves plainly visible outside the jail yard gate and for several yards down C Street suggested that confederates had been waiting to aid the escapees.

By 10:00 a.m., Sheriff Sam McDowell and a posse of fourteen mounted men were scouring the roads for traces of the fleeing prisoners. Telegrams were sent to all local railroad stations offering $100 rewards and describing the four fugitives. Fowler was described as a short, heavy-set man with a light complexion and "shocky" hair. Young was five feet, eight inches tall, with "a peculiar drawn expression around his mouth," which gave him the appearance of sneering when he talked. Shock and Hair—regarded as minor criminals—were mostly ignored by the newspapers, which considered their recapture imminent. (In fact, after their reported escape, the two would never be mentioned again in the local newspapers.) But the *Daily Sun* warned, "Young and Fowler are shrewd criminals and their capture is doubtful."

The escapees' trail seemed to lead east toward El Cajon. A letter found in the road from Theodore Fowler taunted the pursuers. "If you send any one after me, don't send Charlie Murphy, for I will kill him on sight." Fowler, it seemed, had a history with Murphy, one of Sheriff McDowell's deputies.

Convicted cattle rustler and jail breaker Theodore Fowler. *Courtesy of Terry Chaffee, great-nephew of Theodore Fowler.*

Three days after the escape, McDowell and Murphy spotted Fowler in rough terrain near Jamacha. "Fowler made a desperate resistance," reported the *Union*. "Jumping from his horse [he] disappeared in the brush, firing four shots at Murphy while running." While the officers "pressed him hard," it was growing dark, and the chase was abandoned until morning. The next day, Fowler was gone without a trace.

The deputies had better luck with John Young. In early May, they received word that Mexican authorities had captured the fugitive near Ensenada. A "kid-gloved sort of chap," Young gave deputies little trouble as he was brought back to San Diego.

Mexico also appeared to be the refuge of Theodore Fowler. Throughout the summer, rumors drifted back to San Diego that Fowler had taken up horse theft as an occupation in the mountains near El Compadre, southeast of Tecate. San Diego constable James Russell caught up with the fugitive in late August after Mexican soldiers arrested him for kidnapping a fifteen-year-old girl.

Fowler was taken to Ensenada and lodged in an adobe jailhouse. He escaped the first night—leaving behind a sleeping dummy in his cell made from his hat, boots and overalls. But this time, Fowler would not go far. Pursuers captured him the next day—barefoot and exhausted—in rough country a few miles away. As he was put on a boat to San Diego, the unrepentant outlaw told his captors that "with a horse and six-shooter he would not have been taken alive."

On November 13, 1888, Theodore Fowler began his ten-year incarceration at the state prison at San Quentin. Only five months later, he attempted to escape. Quickly caught, he was placed in "the Dungeon" for ten days, and an extra year was added to his sentence.

W.E.Hale, Warden
J.V.Ellis, Clerk

OFFICE OF
WARDEN

STATE PRISON AT SAN QUENTIN

CALIFORNIA

DIRECTORS
EDGAR J DEPUE. PRESIDENT.
J.H.NEFF.   CHARLES SONNTAG.
R.T.DEVLIN DANIEL E.HAYES

P.O.ADDRESS.
San Quentin, Cal. Sept.22nd,1893.

Hon.H.H.Markham,Governor,
        Sacramento,California.

My Dear Sir:-

            Enclosed I hand you papers· in the case of Theodore
Fowler who has applied for a pardon.   As you will observe by Sec.
Ellis' letter,the Board,at the regular meeting yesterday,recommend-
ed that a commutation be granted by which he will be liberated immediately.   If the above recommendation meets with your approval
and you conclude to issue a commutation,kindly telegraph me on
Saturday,as I expect that his brother-in-law will be here on the
next day.

            I would state in this connection that in a conversation with
Dr.Mansfield yesterday,he informed me that,at best,Fowler has but
a few months to live.

                    Yours very truly,

                                W.E.Hale

                                Warden.

Dying from tuberculosis, Theodore Fowler petitioned California governor Henry Markham for a pardon. The warden of San Quentin endorsed Fowler's release. *Courtesy of California State Archives.*

   Working in the jute mill in the cold, damp climate of San Quentin, Fowler's health began to decline. He applied for a pardon in March 1892, arguing that his ten-year sentence for stealing a cow was excessive and based solely on his prior conviction for a similar crime. The application was denied.

The next summer, as an inmate in the consumptive ward at San Quentin, he tried again. When the prison doctor determined that Fowler was dying from tuberculosis, frantic letters to the governor from Fowler's family appealed for mercy. "His Race is Run and he has but a Short time to Spend on this earth," wrote his sister. Governor Henry H. Markham granted the pardon on September 13, 1893. Theodore Fowler was released to his family in San Luis Obispo, where he died two months later at age twenty-nine.

THE CARNEGIE LIBRARY ART ROBBERY

As a target for art thieves, the public library would seem an unlikely place. Nevertheless, janitor Robert Butler had an unwelcome surprise when he opened the doors of the library on Friday morning, February 5, 1909. As Butler climbed the stairs to the art gallery on the second floor, he was shocked by the sight of empty picture frames strewn along the baseboards. Fifteen oil paintings on loan from prominent local artists had disappeared.

"VALUABLE PAINTINGS STOLEN FROM LIBRARY" screamed the headline in the *San Diego Sun*. The works of art were part of the "midwinter exhibit" by the San Diego Art Association, the city's first organization for local artists. The downtown Carnegie Library was a popular location for exhibiting art. Open twelve hours a day during the week and three hours on Sunday, hundreds of San Diegans viewed the art each day.

The doors and windows were locked "the same as I left them Thursday night," janitor Butler told the police. Butler guessed that a burglar had concealed himself in a storeroom before the library closed at 9:00 p.m. With the whole night ahead of him, the thief then leisurely removed the paintings from their stretchers, rolled them up and strolled out the library doors.

The *Los Angeles Times* offered a different theory, reporting that thieves "drove up to the building with a wagon, entered through a window, loaded the wagon and drove off." City librarian Hannah Davison declared the value of the paintings were in the neighborhood of $3,000.

Victimized artists included Albert R. Valentien, Mary B. Williams, Charles A. Fries and seven others. Valentien surmised that the thieves were connoisseurs who intended to sell the paintings "in the east." But he was optimistic that the art would be found soon, "as they are so well known that it would be difficult to dispose of them." The police were less confident, telling the *Evening Tribune*, "It is doubtful whether any of the pictures will be recovered."

The Carnegie Library often exhibited fine art on the second floor of its building at Eighth and E Streets. *Courtesy of Special Collections, San Diego Public Library.*

To find any news of the stolen canvases, the San Diego Police Department flooded U.S cities on both coasts with circulars, describing each painting, the title and artist. In the meantime, the San Diego Art Association urged the immediate hiring of a night watchman, warning that without such protection, "artists and other owners of valuable property will not be willing to make loans for purposes of exhibition."

Two days after the discovery of the thefts, janitor Butler found an unlatched window leading to the basement in the library. The window, seemingly locked when Butler and police detectives examined the building after the thefts, had been temporarily secured by someone. "It is barely possible," Butler told a reporter from the *San Diego Union*, "that the thief used the curtain cord as a wedge by which to close the window and make it appear as though the catch had been used."

Police now theorized that the thief had rigged the window frame one day and then returned at night "to throw the window wide open." Suspicious marks on the windowsill appeared to be scuffs from shoes. The detectives decided the thief had "crawled through, jumped to the floor, closed the window behind him, went up into the gallery, gathered up his pictures and made his exit in the same way."

The San Diego Public Library building, financed by Andrew Carnegie, opened in 1902 and served the growing city for the next fifty years. *Courtesy of Special Collections, San Diego Public Library.*

Discovery of the thief's likely entrance site did not get detectives any closer to an arrest or recovery of the stolen paintings. But after weeks of chasing dead ends, the detectives got a lucky break.

A burglar had recently been arrested in Santa Ana for robbing a gun store. After a quick trial, twenty-three-year-old John R. Keene began a five-year sentence at San Quentin. Shortly after his conviction, Orange County sheriff Theo Lacey found a receipt among Keene's effects for a package stored at the Union Warehouse Company in Los Angeles.

Lacey called on Sheriff Bill Hammell of Los Angeles, and the two men visited the Union Warehouse. With the receipt in hand, they found a large package of stolen goods, including fifteen oil paintings in one large roll. The sheriffs immediately recognized the art as work described in the circular sent two months earlier by the San Diego police.

On April 7, two months after robbery, Charles Fries took the train to Los Angeles and personally identified the stolen paintings belonging to him and the other artists. San Diego Police Chief William Neely brought the paintings back to San Diego ten days later.

Art Association president Daniel Cleveland declared that his organization was overjoyed with the news. "These pieces," he said, "were of inestimable value to their owners and the association would never have recovered from the shock had they not been recovered."

MUTINY ON THE *DUDHOPE*

The arrival of the British tall ship *Dudhope* in San Diego harbor on November 30, 1914, was an impressive sight. With its "massive yards and mast and the white sails hauled tight by the brisk breeze," the *Union* called the two-thousand-ton ship "a "marine spectacle."

The steel-hulled bark had the historic distinction of being the last cargo-carrying windjammer to enter San Diego via the storied Cape Horn route. But the ship would be better remembered for a surprising mutiny.

When the *Dudhope* arrived in San Diego, the crew was startled to learn that since its departure from Hamburg, Germany, in early July, war had begun

The British bark *Dudhope* is shown at full sail outside San Diego Bay. *Courtesy of Maritime Museum of San Diego.*

in Europe. The ship's thirty-five-man crew, which included nine Germans, took the news quietly. The *Dudhope*'s British master, Francis Hodgins, was confident there would be no trouble with his men.

Captain Hodgins had actually learned of the Great War several weeks earlier. Off the west coast of South America on the night of October 21, the *Dudhope* had passed a French steamship that flashed the coded news with a lamp: "ENGLAND AND GERMANY AT WAR CAUTION." Only Hodgins and his first mate saw the message, which they cautiously kept to themselves.

In San Diego, the *Dudhope* anchored at Spreckels' Wharf to unload a cargo of iron ore and fertilizer and resupply the ship for its next port of call, Seattle. But the seamen were restless. Nearly one-third of the mostly European crew demanded their wages and release, fearing that with the world at war they were "liable to capture or death by the sinking of the English ship."

A retired American naval officer, William R. Cushman, agreed to represent ten of the men in U.S. District Court. In a suit filed on behalf of the sailors from Norway, Sweden, Germany, Denmark and Finland, Cushman argued that men who signed ship's articles in a time of peace could not be "compelled to undergo the hazard of war."

The attorney demanded that the *Dudhope* be confiscated and sold if necessary to pay off the sailors. "The men want to return to their homes," Cushman said, "and do not care to take any chance of being picked up by a German or Austrian cruiser or sent to the bottom."

The court was sympathetic and, on December 10, gave Captain Hodgins twenty-four hours to pay and let the men go or the ship would remain tied up in San Diego. With their liberation pending, most of the men returned to ship. But four German seamen deserted. Suspicious of their captain's intentions, the sailors disappeared in San Diego.

At 5:00 a.m. the next morning, Captain Hodgins called every man on the ship to his cabin. As the sailors stood at attention, Hodgins reminded them that they had all signed three-year contacts in Hamburg months earlier. He then read a few sentences from admiralty law and asked the men if they had any complaints about their treatment aboard ship. The men said no; they had no fault with the ship, the officers or the food.

"Then we shall go about our regular duties," the captain said. "Do any of you refuse, remembering that to do so constitutes a state of mutiny?" Seven sailors stepped forward and declared they would not obey orders.

"Bellowing like a bull," Captain Hodgins ordered his first mate to bring handcuffs. "Without more ado he clapped the manacles on the wrists of each of the mutinous seamen and ordered them confined in the forecastle, the Germans on one side, the Scandinavians on the other."

Hodgins immediately took his ship out to sea, anchoring three miles off shore in view of the Hotel del Coronado. He then took a boat ashore to take care of last-minute business, including the recruitment of several sailors to replace his missing Germans.

Later in the day, the captain was served by a deputy U.S. marshal with a citation ordering him to appear in district court on December 28 to answer the charges of his crew. Hodgins pointed out that his ship was anchored in international waters. He ignored the summons and returned to the ship. That night, the *Dudhope* weighed anchor and sailed away, headed for Seattle.

Left behind were four unrepentant German seamen. The sailors found refuge with a local grocer, a German immigrant named Fred Eickmeyer, who hid the men on his ranch near Otay until the *Dudhope* sailed. Two of the deserters eventually enlisted in the U.S. Navy. Another joined the crew of John D. Spreckels's yacht, the *Venetian*. The fourth man found work in a San Diego tuna cannery.

The *Dudhope* sailed to the northwest as planned and then, carrying American wheat loaded in Portland, headed home to England. But the ship would not survive the war. On July 15, 1917, the *Dudhope* met a German U-boat two hundred miles from the coast of Ireland. Captain Richard Hartmann captured the windjammer, set the crew adrift in lifeboats and then sank the ship with his deck guns.

Captain Hartmann would get his comeuppance less than two months later. Off the coast of France, *U-49* fired two torpedoes at the English freighter *British Transport*. When the torpedoes missed, the freighter turned and rammed the submarine, sinking the U-boat with all hands.

Shootout in Downtown

The scene at Fifth Avenue and F Street was like an episode of violence from a western movie or four hours of street fighting from a war. Only the uniforms were wrong—and the "enemy" was a single gunman.
—San Diego Union, *April 9, 1965*

About 10:00 a.m. on the rainy morning of April 8, 1965, twenty-eight-year-old Robert Anderson entered a pawnshop at the corner of Fifth Avenue and F Street and asked to see a rifle. Store manager Louis Richards, sixty-one,

From the cover of a beverage truck in the middle of Fifth Avenue, policemen eyed the scene at the Hub Jewelry & Loan Co. *Courtesy of the San Diego Police Museum.*

handed the young man a 30.06 Remington and began writing up a bill of sale. But Anderson surprised the manager by grabbing a box of ammunition and quickly loading the rifle.

"If you want it take it," Richards said. Instead, Anderson raised the gun and fired, fatally wounding Richards. A second store employee, Theodore Swienty, sixty-three, raced upstairs and hid in a small room. While Anderson searched for Swienty, the police arrived and surrounded the pawnshop.

The four-hour shootout at the Hub Jewelry & Loan Co. at 771 Fifth Avenue would be the biggest gun battle ever seen in downtown San Diego. In the aftermath, it would spur the creation of the city's first police SWAT (Special Weapons and Tactics) team. Significantly, *People v. Anderson* would lead to a landmark decision by the state Supreme Court in 1972 that banned the death penalty in California.

The gunman, Robert Page Anderson, was a part-time janitor with a history of drug abuse and scuffles with the law. Raised by his aged grandmother after his parents abandoned him, he was recalled as "a nice little kid" by a neighbor. But others remembered young Anderson for his volatile temper.

As more than sixty policemen armed with shotguns and service revolvers took positions facing the pawnshop, Anderson hurriedly loaded guns taken from the store's huge weapons inventory. "He's got all the guns in the world in that pawnshop," a policeman grumbled, "and the place is probably loaded with ammunition."

To break open windows for tear gas shells, the police hurled Coke bottles from the cover of a beverage truck parked in the middle of Fifth Avenue. Tear gas was then fired into the store, but high winds blew most of the fumes back into a swelling crowd of onlookers.

Reporters from the *Union* and *Evening Tribune* covered the action while crouched in the doorway of the Hi-Life Bar on F Street. Robert Crandall, editor of the *San Diego Independent*, moved close to the scene but fell with an apparent heart attack. A *Union* photographer and a policeman dragged Crandall away and tried to revive him, but he would be pronounced dead at the hospital.

Shortly before noon, the police borrowed an armored money car and backed it up close to the store. Firing shotguns and a submachine gun from the rear of the vehicle, they raked the store from floor to ceiling. Apparently unhurt, Anderson responded with small arms fire.

About 1:15 p.m., it began raining heavily. Hundreds of wet spectators continued to gawk at the action. A mailman, oblivious to the scene, walked down F Street delivering his mail. Two officers grabbed the man and hustled him away. City meter maids ignored the action and continued to write overtime parking tickets on cars.

Heavily armed policemen took firing positions on F Street facing the Hub Jewelry store. *Courtesy of the San Diego Police Museum.*

At 1:30 p.m., a policeman with a bullhorn warned Anderson that grenades would be fired if he didn't drop his weapons and come out. Minutes later, a navy gunner's mate, Frank Morales, lobbed a concussion grenade into the store. Fire and glass spewed from the windows. The policemen charged into the building.

Anderson was nowhere in sight. "He's upstairs," a patrolman yelled when Anderson began firing down on the officers. Morales threw a second grenade into a mezzanine above the shop.

Sergeant Allen D. Brown worked his way up a smoke-filled stairway. He met Anderson face to face in a dark corridor. The gunman had a revolver in his hand, but he had loaded it with the wrong ammunition. The gun clicked twice but misfired. Brown emptied his shotgun and downed Anderson.

The sergeant found Theodore Swienty hiding under a bed in severe shock. He helped the clerk out of the store and then returned to the wounded Anderson. The gunman had been shot in the abdomen and both arms and appeared to be dying. Taken to the county hospital, he would recover after extensive surgery.

At his trial, Anderson offered little for his defense, claiming at first that a "masked man" had entered the shop and killed the manager. Later, he would say that Richards and Swienty had uttered racial slurs when he—a young black man—entered the shop to pawn a diamond ring. "They talked kind of funny like they didn't want to serve me."

A jury of six men and six women deliberated for nine hours before convicting Anderson of the first-degree murder of Louis Richards and the attempted murders of Theodore Swienty and Sergeant Allen Brown. He was sentenced to die in the gas chamber, but in the next seven years, he would survive three dates with the executioner.

For his last appeal, the American Civil Liberties Union pressed the argument that capital punishment violated the state constitution's prohibition of "cruel and unusual punishment." In a historic ruling delivered on February 18, 1972, the California Supreme Court struck down the death sentence statute, declaring it "incompatible with the dignity of man and the judicial process."

The death sentences of Anderson and 105 other condemned prisoners—including killers such as Charles Manson and Sirhan Sirhan—were lifted and commuted to life in prison. The death penalty statute in California would later be restored by constitutional amendment.

Robert Page Anderson was released on parole in 1976 after serving eleven years at San Quentin. He moved to Seattle, earned a community college degree and counseled juvenile delinquents for a time. At last report, he was living alone in a tiny apartment in Seattle on a Social Security pension.

WATER FOR A THIRSTY REGION

THE ENGINEERING MARVEL OF SWEETWATER DAM

Under balmy skies and amidst brilliant flowers the celebration of the completion of the National City waterworks and the great Sweetwater Dam was held at National City yesterday. It was a success in every way, and April 19 will ever be a red letter day in the history of the rising young city down the bay.
—San Diego Union, *April 20, 1888*

Jubilation greeted the opening of the Sweetwater Dam in the spring of 1888. On the heels of the great land boom of the eighties, National City and the South Bay reveled in the completion of an engineering marvel—the tallest masonry arch dam in the United States, which created San Diego County's first large reservoir of water, an essential key to the region's growth and prosperity.

National City pioneer Frank Kimball had acquired the site for the dam twenty-one years earlier. By 1880, the San Diego Land and Town Company owned the franchise. This land syndicate (and subsidiary of the Santa Fe Railroad) owned thousands of acres of agricultural land but found its property almost worthless without access to a reliable water supply.

SWEETWATER DAM!

DAILY! Train Leaves Foot of Fifth Street, SAN DIEGO, at 9:30 A. M., **DAILY!**

ARRIVE AT NATIONAL CITY AT 10:05.

Leaving National City the tourist enters beautiful Chula Vista, with its thousands of acres of orange and lemon orchards, handsome villa homes and an endless vista of valley, mountain, bay and grand old ocean. Then comes the city of Otay, nestling snuggly in one of the prettiest valleys in all California. At 11:07 the train arrives at Tia Juana, where the excursionist is given fifty minutes to visit the Mexican Custom House, Curiosity stores, and other places of interest in Old Mexico. Beautiful onyx and quaint Mexican curios can be purchased there at reasonable prices.

Leaving TIA JUANA at 12.00 noon, the train returns to National City, where good lunch may be procured at the International hotel, or visit the beautiful orchards at Olivewood. Leaving National City at 2:20 p. m., passing through the beautiful Sweetwater Valley, skirting numerous vineyards and orange groves, and at 3:00 o'clock reaches the famous

SWEETWATER DAM ᵃⁿᵈ SWEETWATER RESERVOIR

BUILT BY SAN DIEGO LAND & TOWN CO.

Length at base	76 feet	Thickness at base	46 feet	Height of dam from bed rock ... 90 feet
Length at top	396 feet	Thickness at top	12 feet	Reservoir covers ... 1000 acres

Constructed of Solid Granite and Portland Cement. Commenced Nov. 17, 1886. Completed April 7, 1888. Cost $1,000,000.

Returning the train will arrive at National City at 4:14 P. M., and San Diego at 4:45 P. M.

☞ For Further Information and Tickets, apply at Santa Fe and Southern Pacific Ticket Offices, all Hotel Offices in San Diego, San Diego Drug Co., cor. D and Fifth, or at Station Foot of Fifth Street.

FARE:

From SAN DIEGO, for round trip, $1.00.   From NATIONAL CITY, for round trip, 80 cts.

Special ∴ Saturday ∴ Excursions ∴ to ∴ Oneonta ∴ Sanitarium!

For Particulars inquire of Agent foot of Fifth Street.

RECORD PRINT   E A. HORNBECK, Superintendent.

The successful Sweetwater Dam and reservoir became an instant tourist attraction after it opened in 1888. *Courtesy of Special Collections, San Diego Public Library.*

Investment potential, more than the needs of people, spurred the start of dam construction on the Sweetwater in November 1886.

The Sweetwater River (known as *El Dulce* in the Spanish days of the early 1800s) is an intermittent stream. Though often dry in the summer and fall, heavy winter storms could produce quick, violent floods, creating a roaring river heard for miles as it raced to the sea.

To capture this flow for irrigation and drinking water, construction of a dam began in a narrow gorge seven miles from the river's mouth. A level valley behind the dam provided a site for a reservoir. Rushing to build the dam quickly to stimulate land sales, the San Diego Land and Town Company ignored the need for preliminary studies and hired engineer F.E. Brown, who had recently built a small rock dam at Bear Canyon in the San Bernardino Mountains.

Brown designed a thin, fifty-foot-tall concrete dam, reinforced on the upstream side by a dirt embankment. The project started off badly. After two months of work, a frustrated Frank Kimball would write in his journal, "Am thoroughly disgusted with the entire management and the method of construction and I believe the dam cannot stand."

The land syndicate agreed. Brown was fired and replaced by James Dix Schulyer, thirty-nine, a professional civil engineer with expertise in irrigation systems. Schulyer immediately rejected the old design and began work on a sixty-foot-tall, masonry dam that would impound more water in a larger reservoir.

"To meet a pressing demand for water, the new dam was hastily run up," recalled Schulyer. By June, the dam had hit the sixty-foot target, but Schulyer suggested going higher when his studies determined that a ninety-foot dam would impound five times the water of the smaller design. The San Diego Land and Town Company endorsed the added expenditure, and the work sped forward.

Schulyer's masonry dam was built with huge stones—some weighing several tons—quarried from rock cliffs eight hundred feet downstream. The stone was hauled to the work site in horse-drawn wagons and then hoisted aloft and set in position from wooden derricks mounted on the wall of the dam. Animal power alone worked the derricks, "as fuel was scarce and dear." Portland cement and river sand composed the mortar.

Manpower needs were considerable, and Schulyer complained that "labor of all kinds was difficult to obtain and hard to hold." Wages in booming Southern California were high for the day. Laborers earned up to $2.50 per day on the Sweetwater project, while their foremen made between $4.00 and $6.00. Stone masons made $5.00, carpenters and blacksmiths $4.00. The most specialized workers, the machinists, earned a lucrative $1.00 per hour. Schulyer proudly pointed out that "there was no loss of human life and no serious accident during the work."

The dam was finished on April 7, 1888, after only sixteen months of construction. The final structure had a 46-foot base, narrowing to 12 feet at the top. The dam was 90 feet tall with a top length of 396 feet. The seven-hundred-

The Sweetwater Dam overflowing on March 29, 1909. *Courtesy of Special Collections, San Diego Public Library.*

acre lake behind the dam was three miles long and three-quarters of a mile wide. The builders boasted that the lake's six billion gallons of water was "sufficient for 500,000 people" or would "cover 20,000 acres twelve inches in depth."

Ironically, the Sweetwater reservoir was mostly dry at first. When an upstream landowner complained that the lake was flooding his property, the courts ordered the San Diego Land and Town Company to release water, lowering the reservoir to a fraction of its capacity. The plaintiff, rancher George Neal, would battle the aggravated land syndicate for two years before settling for $80,000.

The strength and capacity of Sweetwater Dam received its first test in January 1895. Five inches of rain fell on two consecutive days and filled the reservoir to overflowing. For forty hours, water cascaded over the top of the dam at a depth of two feet. The dam survived, but the foundation and abutments were weakened. Engineers repaired the damage and raised the dam two feet. In 1910–11, the dam was raised another fifteen feet, increasing the potential capacity of Sweetwater Reservoir by 70 percent.

The dam's biggest test came with the great Rainmaker Flood of January 1916, which dropped twenty inches of rain on Sweetwater. The dam was overtopped to a depth of three and a half feet. Once again, Schulyer's dam stood up to the torrent, but the abutments on both sides washed away, leaving gaping channels for the floodwater to race through. Tragically, eight people died in the downstream flood.

Over the years, several rehabilitations have preserved and improved the Sweetwater structure and raised its height to its current 127 feet. For 120 years, the Sweetwater Dam has served the South Bay communities. On April 7, 2006, the American Society of Civil Engineers officially recognized this remarkable dam as a National Historic Landmark.

THE RAINMAKER

The city council signed a contract yesterday with Hatfield, the Moisture Accelerator. He has promised to fill Morena reservoir to overflowing by December 20, 1916, for $10,000. All the councilmen are in favor of the contract except Fay, who says it's rank foolishness.
—San Diego Union, *December 14, 1915*

Councilman Fay had it right. But by the end of 1915, San Diego was in its fifth year of drought. The city reservoirs of Morena and Otay were nearly empty. With water supplies threatened, the nervous city councilmen gave verbal acceptance to the offer of a "Rainmaker," Charles M. Hatfield, who boldly pledged to "fill the Morena reservoir to overflowing."

Hatfield, who once earned a living selling sewing machines door to door, had found rainmaking a lucrative occupation. Throughout Southern California and dry locales ranging from Texas to Montana, farmers clamored for Hatfield's services. He usually timed his jobs to coincide with the rainy season. When the rains came, Hatfield took the credit.

On New Year's Day 1916, Charles and his younger brother Paul went to work. From a wooden tower they built near Lake Morena, the brothers brewed a blend of chemicals designed to "enhance moisture." One observer recalled his visit to the scene: "I was startled by a sudden view of what looked like an oil tower on the heights above Morena basin. In the sky appeared puffs of smoke, and I heard explosions...It was Hatfield, shooting bombs, exploding them in an incantation aimed at wringing moisture from the air."

Fumes wafted skyward. And on January 10, it started to rain.

In the next two weeks, more than seventeen inches of rain fell in the mountains. The reservoirs filled, and streams overran their banks. The San Diego River rose, and Mission Valley flooded. The Tijuana River carried

The rainmaker Charles M. Hatfield would never reveal the secrets of his chemical blend designed to "enhance moisture." *Courtesy of Special Collections, San Diego Public Library.*

away the farming settlement of Little Landers, north of the Mexican border. Roads and bridges disappeared.

A second storm arrived on January 25, bringing another foot of rain. Two days later, water flowed over the top of Sweetwater Dam and then broke through the abutments on the sides of the dam.

But the most dramatic story was occurring farther south at the Lower Otay Dam. Just after 6:00 p.m. on January 27, floodwaters topped the dam. "The tension was so great," an engineer would later report, "that the steel [core] torc from the top at the center, and the dam opened outward like a pair of gates." A wall of water raced downstream through the Otay Valley,

Water for a Thirsty Region

Above: A flooded Mission Valley in January 1916. *Courtesy of Special Collections, San Diego Public Library.*

Below: Powerful floodwaters washed downstream a huge chunk of boiler plate steel from the core of the broken Otay Dam. *Courtesy of Special Collections, San Diego Public Library.*

sweeping away houses, bridges, railroad tracks and livestock and killing at least fourteen people.

Oblivious to the scale of the havoc and with their mission complete at Morena, Charles and Paul Hatfield walked the sixty miles back to San Diego and presented city hall with their bill for $10,000. City attorney Terence Cosgrove showed the brothers the door, explaining there was no written contract for their "rainmaking" and the deluge was "an act of God."

The brothers seethed for nearly a year and then filed suit on December 2. Cosgrove offered to settle with Hatfield if he accepted responsibility for $3,500,000 in damages caused by the flooding. The rainmaker declined the offer. His suit would linger for over twenty years before dismissal by the San Diego Superior Court in 1938.

Charles M. Hatfield eventually returned to selling sewing machines. He would go to his grave, in 1958, insisting that his efforts had brought beneficial rain, not destruction. "The rain of 1916 was an act of Hatfield," he declared, "not an act of God."

WOODEN PIPES TO THE CITY

There wasn't a lawn in the city. But some people went without baths so they could water their pet shrubs. Everybody with money left town. Those who remained became water experts.
—*Fred Heilbron, city councilman and water crusader*

With a population of fewer than eighteen thousand at the turn of the century, San Diego's water needs should have been simple. But after several years of drought in the late 1890s, the thirsty city struggled for a reliable water supply.

Even the great wooden flume built in 1888 that brought rainwater from the Cuyamaca Mountains to San Diego was running almost dry after three years of rainfall that averaged barely five inches. The San Diego Water Company maintained a meager supply in 1900 by pumping from wells in the bed of the San Diego River in Mission Valley.

To ensure dependable sources, the City of San Diego looked to the private companies that supplied all the region's water. In late 1900, the city council approved the purchase of the twenty-eight-year-old San Diego Water Company, and the distributing system of the Southern California Mountain Water Company for water delivered within San Diego. City voters passed bond measures the following spring to finance the purchases.

Water for a Thirsty Region

The Southern California Mountain Water Company, owned by capitalists John D. Spreckels and Elisha S. Babcock, had recently built the Lower Otay Dam (1897), started work on the Morena Dam and planned construction on Barrett Dam. The *Union* predicted the string of new reservoirs—perhaps the largest water project in the United States at the time—would create "an immense storage capacity" with a "practically exhaustless" water supply.

To get that water to San Diego, the Mountain Water Company began construction of a pipeline. Remarkably, the pipe would be made of wood— nearly twenty miles of it—stretching from Otay to San Diego, with additional branch lines to supply farmers in the Otay Valley and residents of Coronado.

Wood-stave pipes were the modern method for bringing water to cities. The first public water system in America had brought water to Boston, Massachusetts, through wood pipe in 1652. Two and a half centuries later, the technique was still state of the art. "It is common knowledge that wood pipe," noted the American Water Works Association in 1922, "buried in the ground or kept saturated with water, has an indefinitely long life."

For the San Diego project, engineers designed forty-inch-diameter pipe made from Humboldt County redwood. The pipeline would run northward from Lower Otay for nineteen miles, ending at a new city reservoir being built at Chollas Heights. From Chollas, the water would run four miles northwest through cast-iron pipes to the city filtration plant at University Heights at Howard Avenue and Oregon Street. There, the water would be aerated in a fountain and then piped to city users.

Construction began in December 1900, when laborers from the Mountain Water Company began building tunnels and trestles in preparation for the redwood pipe, which was being cured at Coronado. The contract for trimming the lumber into pipe staves went to the Russ Lumber Company of San Diego.

Building the pipeline required a series of work camps that moved along as the conduit was laid. Tents, cookhouses and livestock corrals supplied the laborers who earned $2.00 a day, minus $4.50 a week for board. The poorly paid work was manual and low-tech. Mules dragged excavating "machines," and horse teams delivered materials by wagon.

With the trenches dug, the workers assembled the redwood pipe like a cooper building a barrel. The tapered, wedge-shaped staves—twelve to sixteen feet in length—were formed into a cylinder held together by iron bands. Water pressure usually kept the pipe tight, though blown-out staves and broken bands could create spectacular geysers. Properly maintained, engineers expected the wood pipe to last about twenty-five years.

San Diego's wooden pipelines could create spectacular geysers of water when they began to fail. *Courtesy of Historical Collection, San Diego Water Department.*

"Neither men nor money will be spared in hurrying the water into San Diego at the earliest possible moment," reported the *Union* on January 1, 1901. By late summer, the pipeline stretched nine miles. Water to Bonita and Chula Vista arrived in August to irrigate the lemon and orange orchards. The *Union* heralded "the great success which attended this first delivery" and predicted the pipeline would soon reach the city limits of San Diego.

There was also fast progress building a new city reservoir in Chollas Heights to serve as the terminus of the pipeline. An earth-fill dam with a steel and masonry core was built over the summer of 1901. The reservoir held enough water to supply the city for two months.

But the water to fill Chollas was slow in coming. The Mountain Water Company finished its pipeline to Bonita and then stopped. Decent rainfall in 1901 diminished demand for water from Lower Otay, and the pipeline project lagged. In the meantime, San Diego's first municipal water department—organized in August 1901—continued to rely on supplies from the San Diego Flume Company and well water from Mission Valley.

The City of San Diego agreed to a new contract with the Mountain Water Company in the fall of 1905, to purchase water from Otay for the price of four cents per one thousand gallons—a price low enough for the city to close its Mission Valley pumping plant and end the purchase of water from the flume company. Work started up again on the wooden conduit to Chollas and the branch line to Coronado.

The completed pipeline opened on August 13, 1906. In a grand public ceremony at University Heights, Mayor John Sehon turned a six-foot-long ceremonial key, which opened a gate to release water that had traveled twenty miles via redwood pipe. Drinking glasses of Otay water were passed among assembled dignitaries. Unfortunately, the soil filters were not working. The cloudy water was politely overlooked and "its excellent quality was generally commented on."

A segment of redwood pipeline being assembled near Chollas Lake in 1906. *Courtesy of Historical Collection, San Diego Water Department.*

San Diego's wooden pipeline lasted until 1930, when it was replaced by a new pipeline of cast iron and steel. By that time, the city's population had grown to nearly 148,000, and plans were being made for a massive reservoir at El Capitan in a new attempt to address the insatiable demand for water in San Diego.

A DAM FIASCO

To look at it now, solidly in place, you would never know its disturbed history. The broken course of the Sutherland project is one of those fantastic things that could only happen here.
—*Shelley Higgins, former city attorney, in* This Fantastic City

In February 1927, on remote canyon land ten miles northeast of Ramona, the City of San Diego began construction of the Sutherland Dam. Only eighteen months later, the ill-starred project would end—victimized by a series of problems including design errors, financial difficulties and political squabbling. The site of the "dam fiasco" would remain untouched for the next twenty-five years.

The dam on San Ysabel Creek—named for a local rancher, John P. Sutherland—was intended to capture rainfall from the San Dieguito watershed, which averages thirty inches a year. Billions of gallons of water that normally flowed to the ocean each year would be preserved in the new reservoir. Construction funds would come from a $2 million bond measure passed by San Diego voters on October 19, 1926. Less than half of that amount was designated to build Sutherland Dam.

The construction firm of Edwards, Wildey & Dixon—low-bid contractors from Los Angeles—began building a road to the isolated site as soon as the ink dried on its $885,000 contract. Heavy rains promptly washed out the roadwork; the winter of 1927 would be one of the wettest on record. Undeterred, the contractors rebuilt the road and began work on the dam's foundation.

But another problem emerged. Engineers reported that borings for the dam's base indicated "a highly fissured condition of the foundation rock." Deeper digging would be required to reach sound bedrock. Cost estimates began to rise. Supervising engineer J.W. Williams warned that total expenses might exceed $1.7 million.

By summer, rumors were flying that the foundation site was unsuitable and the dam could not be built there at any cost. A panel of consulting

Huge concrete abutments were left unfinished when work on the Sutherland Dam was abandoned. *Courtesy of Historical Collection, San Diego Water Department.*

engineers visited the site and suggested that a better foundation site could be found upstream.

And so the entire project was moved seven hundred yards up the creek and restarted. But the second site presented new difficulties. Now the entire dam would need to be three hundred feet longer to span a wider canyon area. Cost estimates soared to over $2 million.

By the summer of 1928, the slow-moving Sutherland venture was nearly bankrupt. In desperation, the city council turned to a water engineer it had once fired: Hiram N. Savage. The builder of several San Diego projects, including the Lower Otay Dam in 1919 and Barrett Dam in 1922, Savage had vast local experience. But he was also known for his stubbornness and inability to compromise—traits that cost him his job in 1923 when he quarreled with council politicians.

Given a second opportunity in July 1928, Savage's first order of business was an inspection of the Sutherland site. His immediate reaction was harsh criticism of the dam's multiple-arch design. Concrete arch dams had been built successfully before in California. Only ten years earlier, the multiple-arched Hodges Dam in Escondido and Murray Dam in La Mesa were built with the designs of the respected hydraulic engineer John S. Eastwood.

But Savage hated the dams, believing that only his single-arch, monolithic concrete dams were sound. He even warned the city council that Hodges was unsafe and liable to fail at any time. The council was sensitive to any hint of possible dam failure from poor design or construction. Only months earlier, the St. Francis Dam near Los Angeles had collapsed, killing hundreds of people downstream.

On August 13, Savage advised the council that only $100,000 in bond funds remained for a dam he believed would cost an additional $700,000 to complete. With Sutherland only 25 percent complete, work was suspended at the end of the month. Only a caretaker remained at the site.

A year later, a wildfire swept through the Sutherland basin, destroying buildings and equipment and eliminating any hope of restarting the costly project. "All that remains of the city's Sutherland venture," reported the *Union*, "are some concrete buttresses uprearing at the damsite, a pile of reinforced steel shapes rusting on a hillside and an engineer's camp nestled on a hillside."

With Sutherland abandoned, the city took on other water projects. Hiram Savage supervised the construction of the earth-fill El Capitan Dam in 1932–35 (after voters refused to fund his preferred concrete dam in Mission Gorge), and San Vicente Dam was finished in 1943. In 1946, the first Colorado River water came to San Diego via an aqueduct from San Jacinto.

None of these projects was enough to satisfy the water needs of a region that doubled in population size during World War II. A second barrel was planned for the San Diego Aqueduct, and the city took a fresh look at the long-forsaken ruins of the Sutherland project.

In 1952, workers returned to the Sutherland Dam to finish work that had stopped twenty-four years earlier. *Courtesy of Historical Collection, San Diego Water Department.*

"We need that water," declared Ralph Phillips of the Greater San Diego Water Committee. San Diego voters agreed, passing a bond measure in February 1952 for $6.5 million. The bonds restarted work on the old foundations of Sutherland Dam. A second proposition paid for construction of the second barrel for the San Diego Aqueduct.

Finally completed without any hint of the historic complications, Sutherland Dam was dedicated on June 5, 1954. With a crest length of 1,025 feet, Sutherland is the second-longest San Diego dam, surpassed only by El Capitan Dam. When full, 5.25 miles of shoreline surround the reservoir of 556 surface acres of water.

DAMMING MISSION GORGE

One of the biggest hassles we had was trying to keep some of these idiots from building a dam in Mission Gorge...A lot of land would have been flooded—Santee, Lakeside, and about a third of El Cajon Valley would have been a shallow lake.
—Fred A. Heilbron, San Diego city councilman (1919–27)

The city fathers of San Diego were concerned about the water supply. After several years of quiet growth, the population began growing rapidly in the early 1920s—up to 10 percent annually. Would there be enough water to support a growing region? Heavy rainfall in 1921 and 1922 had filled local lakes, but city water engineer Hiram N. Savage sounded an alarm when he announced that the reservoirs had sufficient supply for no more than five years. "It is imperative," he argued, "that the city of San Diego provide promptly, and accomplish not later than 1926, greatly increased reservoir storage."

In August 1921, the city council directed Savage to study the water resources of the San Diego River and report back with recommendations. The engineer returned to the council six months later with a study that identified two "outstanding reservoir basins" on the river: El Capitan, twenty-five miles upstream, and—his strong first choice—Mission Gorge, only seven miles from the city limits.

Savage proposed a concrete dam located about a half mile below the historic Mission Dam. The dam would flood the gorge and the valley beyond, creating a reservoir of ten square miles. The reservoir water could be pumped to the University Heights filtration plant for distribution to the city.

City hydraulic engineer Hiram N. Savage proposed a concrete dam in Mission Gorge on the San Diego River, just below historic Mission Dam. The new dam would have flooded the gorge and the valley beyond, creating a reservoir of ten square miles. *Courtesy of Historical Collection, San Diego Water Department.*

Mission Gorge was perfect as a dam site. A narrow canyon and solid bedrock offered ideal building conditions—the same conditions Savage had used to build successful masonry dams at Lower Otay in 1919 and Barrett in 1922. The El Capitan site, on the other hand, lacked the hard granite foundations necessary for a conventional masonry dam. Only an expensive rock fill dam would do. El Capitan, judged Savage, would be "economically impossible."

The city council was less certain. Mission Gorge may have been an ideal site for a dam, but the reservoir would be shallow and prone to severe evaporation losses. It would also drown a productive agricultural valley. The basin of El Capitan—its supporters argued—drained a massive watershed and would provide a much deeper and larger reservoir.

The chief advocate of the Mission Gorge dam had become a problematic figure, as well. Arrogant and opinionated, Hiram Savage was a difficult man to work with. Land baron Ed Fletcher described him as "old school," a man "positive in his convictions, who would never yield an inch, under any conditions." His refusal to consider alternatives to Mission Gorge infuriated the city council. On June 15, 1923, City Manager Fred Rhodes fired Savage and eliminated his position of hydraulic engineer. When given the news of his discharge in a council meeting, Savage simply replied, "Very well."

With Savage out of the way, the council decided to put the Mission Gorge proposition before the voters. A $3.6 million bond issue was set for an election on September 10, 1924. Councilman Heilbron, City Manager Rhodes and the city attorney, Shelley Higgins, went to work to defeat the measure. "We called mass meetings and we made speeches," recalled Higgins. "We let every San Diegan who would listen, know the disadvantages of the Mission Gorge location."

On election day, the bonds for Mission Gorge were voted down 7,485 to 4,750. A second election held only a month later approved $4.5 million in bonds to build a dam at El Capitan. But even with the endorsement of voters, the project bogged down. For the remainder of the decade, the city fought a costly legal action in the courts to defend the municipality's "paramount rights" to the headwaters of the San Diego River. The case was finally won in 1930.

Remarkably, in June 1929, the city council decided to rehire Hiram Savage. The engineer had always been respected for his expertise and was popular with the public. Deciding it needed Savage to spur progress on urgently needed projects, a new council awarded him a five-year contract.

The return of Savage reignited the old controversy of where to site a dam and reservoir on the San Diego River. Savage strongly reiterated that Mission Gorge provided the quickest and most cost-efficient route to a new reservoir. But other water experts opposed him. Thomas H. King, a civil engineer for the Cuyamaca Water Company, decried the potential flooding of Santee and Lakeside, and M.M. O'Shaughnessy, builder of the dam at Hetch Hetchy in the Yosemite valley, emphasized that El Capitan was the one reservoir on the San Diego River that could store the greatest amount of water with the fewest impacts upon developed lands.

San Diego's newspapers endorsed the Mission Gorge dam. Editorials from the *Union* urged the city to "bank on the engineering advice of Mr. Savage." The *Sun*, claiming it had "never expressed any opinion whatever as to the relative merits" of either site, said the decision should be left to the engineers—namely, Hiram Savage.

The voters had the final word on August 12, 1931. By the narrow margin of 11,152 to 10,281, the people decided for the second time not to fund the Mission Gorge dam. Wiley V. Ambrose, head of a citizens' committee that supported the project, was resigned: "Well, that's that. Evidently the people thought we were wrong. But maybe events will show we were right after all."

Construction of the El Capitan Dam began in December 1931. Hiram Savage would swallow his pride and design his first rock fill dam. He actively supervised the construction but would die of heart failure six months before the dam's completion.

Little noticed in the last weeks of controversy was the fate of 150 Kumeyaay Indians who lived at Capitan Grande—property that would soon be submerged under the new reservoir. The evicted Indians received about $2,400 each for their parcels and moved to new reservation lands at Barona and Viejas.

Completed in 1935, El Capitan was 217 feet high and created a deep reservoir with a water surface up to 1,600 acres. Ironically, most credit for the achievement would go to Hiram Savage, the man who had fought the dam for a decade.

THE NOTORIOUS
STINGAREE

LIQUOR, GUNS AND "RUSSIAN MIKE"

In San Diego's notorious Stingaree district of the 1890s, liquor and violence flowed freely in dozens of saloons south of H Street (Market). One of the more disreputable dives was the Pacific Squadron Saloon on the corner of Fourth and J Streets, where a homicide involving alcohol, a cheap gun and a character named "Russian Mike" drew rapt attention from San Diegans in the spring of 1899.

The Russian-born Michael Rose—known to all as "Russian Mike"—had been a Stingaree terror since his arrival in San Diego in 1884 at age twenty-four. Mike would once claim his father had been killed when he was a child and his sister had raised him until he was nine. After that, he went to sea and saw "every country in the world except Australia."

His wandering stopped in San Diego, where he joined the local Longshoremen's Union but usually earned his meager living as a bartender. The police came to know Mike well. While working at the Eureka saloon at the corner of Second and H—"the resort of dissolute characters and abandoned women of the lowest class," according to the *San Diego Union*—Mike was arrested for the illegal sale of liquor between the hours of midnight and 5:00 a.m. The case was dismissed when the arresting officer admitted in

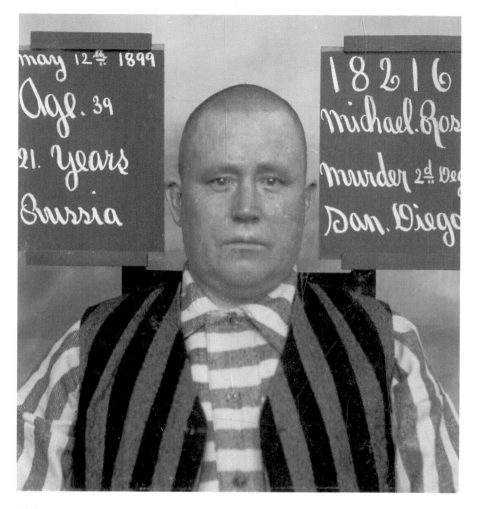

Michael Rose, aka "Russian Mike," in the prison stripes of the state penitentiary at San Quentin. *Courtesy of California State Archives.*

court that he did not know if the "liquor" in glasses was not actually "coffee, tea or sarsaparilla."

Mike was mostly known as a bar fighter—"the hero of many a waterfront melee." Once, on the rare losing end of a brutal battering, he was counseled by Chief of Police Jacob Brenning. "You can blame no one but yourself," the chief said. "My advice is for you to go some place where you are not known, and begin life again in the right way."

Less friendly "advice" came later from policeman James Harris, who clubbed Mike in the head during a barroom altercation in 1897. After the clubbing, Mike would reportedly act strangely at times. One saloon owner warned police to be careful of Russian Mike, since "he was not in his right mind and was liable to kill somebody when he was under the influence of liquor."

On March 27, 1899, Mike lost his job tending bar at the Weeping Willow Saloon. The owner thought Mike could not be depended on. The despondent Russian wandered down the street to Dan Cassidy's Pacific Squadron and began drinking heavily. Later in the evening, Mike started buying drinks for friends. About 10:30 p.m., he passed a silver dollar over the counter for two whiskeys and two beers. Bartender Dan Cassidy returned seventy cents in change.

Trouble began when the heavily inebriated Mike decided Cassidy had not returned his change. "You stole that change from me," he charged the bartender. "I'm not in the habit of stealing change," Cassidy replied, laughing.

When Mike rounded the bar to open the cash register, the forty-three-year-old Cassidy pushed him back, knocking him to the floor. Cassidy pulled Mike to his feet. Mike staggered out the back of the saloon and headed for his room above the Weeping Willow. Grabbing a handgun, he strode purposely back to Cassidy's. "I will fix that man in there, I will blow his whole head off," he muttered as he passed a friend in the alley.

Back inside the Pacific Squadron, Russian Mike showed his gun to Dan Cassidy. The bartender was not impressed. "I am not afraid of that, Mike. You won't shoot."

"I wouldn't?" Mike asked. He raised the gun and fired. Cassidy slumped to the floor without a sound, killed instantly by a bullet above his left eye.

Mike calmly pocketed his gun and walked out of the saloon, only to run into police sergeant José Cota, who happened to be riding by on his horse and had just heard the shot. "What happened?" he asked. "Nothing," Mike replied. "Dan shot himself."

Veteran police sergeant José Cota was quickly on the scene at the Pacific Squadron Saloon, where Daniel Cassidy was shot by Russian Mike. *Courtesy of the San Diego Police Museum.*

Cota surveyed the scene inside and then instructed policeman Harris to retrieve Russian Mike. Harris ran back to the Weeping Willow and arrested him. Sergeant Cota would later find a gun under Mike's pillow—identified as a cheap Harrington & Richardson .38 revolver.

Sitting in a jail cell the next day, Mike claimed to remember nothing: "I had no reasons for shooting Dan; he was one of the best friends I had in this world." But Mike admitted, "I must have done the shooting while I was too drunk to know what I was doing."

A coroner's jury of eleven men was summoned to a local undertaking parlor for an inquest. The bar had been filled that night with customers and several prostitutes who all witnessed the slaying. After listening to the witnesses, the jury ruled: "Death resulted from a mortal wound, caused by a pistol shot fired from a pistol by Michael Rose, otherwise known as Russian Mike."

More eyewitnesses were heard in a packed justice court hearing in April. The testimony was "straightforward" and "very damaging to Russian Mike," concluded a *Union* reporter. The district attorney urged the court to make an example of the murderer.

At trial in superior court in late April, Mike's court-appointed attorney offered an insanity plea. A parade of witnesses claimed Mike had acted oddly since being cracked in the head by Officer Harris two years earlier. The defendant's head was offered as evidence, and each juror carefully felt Mike's skull for the hole he claimed remained from the policemen's blow.

But the jury wasn't buying the insanity claim. After deliberating for fifteen hours, they decided Russian Mike was guilty of second-degree murder. On May 5, Judge John Hughes sentenced Mike to twenty-one years in San Quentin Prison. Four days later, the convicted killer boarded a steamship for the trip north, accompanied by a deputy sheriff. "Russian Mike was in a happy and contented frame of mind when he left," the deputy reported. "He told me that when he is released he will come back to San Diego and try to lead a respectable and upright life."

By 1910, Mike was a free man. The federal census reported him living in San Francisco and working as a street laborer. Twenty years later, his name appeared again in the census, living in a San Francisco hotel and working as a salesman at age seventy.

POLICING THE CITY

What has become of the police force? The archives of the city show that there is such an organization here, yet…the criminal element has been holding high carnival during the last few days, "the guardians of the peace" have done nothing to indicate they are on duty.
—San Diego Union, *August 6, 1887*

Policing a rapidly growing city like San Diego of the mid-1880s was bound to be a problem. Since the arrival of the transcontinental railroad in the city in November 1885, the population had skyrocketed from five thousand to nearly forty thousand in eighteen months.

"The great rush of immigration to this city is bringing with it a gang of lawless ruffians," the *Union* warned. "Burglaries are committed in the heart of the city on bright moonlight nights [and] no arrests are made. We trust that the gang of thieves and thugs that now infest the city will soon be put behind the bars."

Marshal Joseph Coyne commanded a small handful of lawmen challenged by a booming population in the mid-1880s. *Courtesy of the San Diego Police Museum.*

Only "strict police surveillance" would keep crime in check, noted the *Union*. But the handful of constables that once kept order in town was overwhelmed. City Marshal Joe Coyne complained, "I have been a policeman for twenty years, and I never knew a place to be so over-run with men waiting a chance to turn a dishonest penny."

With the boom of the eighties at its height in April 1887, the city trustees approved some help for Coyne with the hiring of eight new policemen, bringing the total force up to about a dozen men. Eventually, over twenty men would be hired. The new officers received German silver stars engraved with the words "Police of San Diego" and equipment that included leather billy clubs, handcuffs and whistles, but no guns. In their blue, brass-buttoned coats and silver stars, the men presented a "formidable appearance."

Marshal Coyne issued strict regulations for his lawmen. Personal conduct rules for men on duty prohibited profane language, smoking and intoxicating liquor. Duties included keeping a "vigilant watch for fires," prevention of "immoderate riding or driving upon public streets" and the reporting of any breach of health laws.

For those on the job in the notorious Stingaree district below H Street (Market), Coyne reminded his men never to leave their assigned posts or visit houses of ill fame ("except in the discharge of their duty") but cautioned them not to allow women of the town to "display themselves at their doors and windows, or solicit customers on the streets."

The officers worked twelve-hour days for $75 a month and paid for their own uniforms. Complaining of their "arduous duties," the policemen requested raises in September 1887. When a petition from eighty-six citizens seconded the request, the monthly pay was raised to $100.

The policemen walked beats and made arrests for mostly petty crimes, including vagrancy and drunkenness, and kept the courthouse jail on D Street (Broadway) filled to capacity. Most offenders were quickly released on bail; ten dollars paid to the clerk on duty was usually sufficient.

The crimes that alarmed the newspapers and civic leaders rarely included felonies. Homicide, rape or grand larceny were infrequently reported. But moral offenses were considered a dire threat to the community, and the newspapers railed against apparent disinterest by the policemen in prosecuting gambling, prostitution and intemperance.

In boomtown San Diego, saloons were required to close each night at 11:00 p.m.—a curfew the police often ignored or allegedly profited from. On one occasion, the *Union* accused two officers of extorting money from Stingaree saloon owners with "subscription lists." As an inducement to "subscribe," officers "intimated that trifling infractions of the 11 o'clock law might, in case liberal donations were made, be winked at."

More contentious was the issue of gambling. A California statute passed in 1885 prohibited professional play of games such as faro, Monte, twenty-one or any game played for money with cards, dice or any device. Violations were punishable by as much as $500 and six months in jail. Of particular concern was the popular saloon game of stud-horse poker. "This pernicious game," argued San Francisco's chief of police in 1884, "fosters idleness, and tempts young men of weak resolution to steal from their employers."

The San Diego police force in 1887. *Courtesy of the San Diego Police Museum.*

Distress over gambling prompted an investigation of the police by the city council in May 1888. Witnesses from Coyne's force offered contradictory testimony about gambling in San Diego saloons. "It was a thing of the past," claimed one officer. But another officer testified that stud-horse poker was running in most all saloons. The witness reminded the councilmen that policemen were not permitted to enter saloons except when called upon to make arrests.

The council also considered allegations of graft among the policemen. The owner of the Hub saloon, on lower Fifth Street, claimed that deputy Larry Barton had demanded $100 as "consideration" to prevent games from being stopped. Barton stoutly denied the charge. His boss, Joe Coyne, told the councilmen that his policemen were instructed to arrest all gamblers. But he admitted he knew of "a gambler named Earp" who had recently defied arrest.

Wyatt Earp, the OK Corral veteran, ran faro games from a Sixth Street saloon near the St. James Hotel. When confronted by an officer, Earp had threatened the lawman, saying that "if he came after his game he would get into his coffin."

Despite testimony about hard cases like Earp, the councilmen seemed satisfied that their police were doing a professional job. The uncomfortable issue of prostitution in the Stingaree was barely addressed by the investigation, though one councilman favored closing the houses of ill repute. Another suggested that a policeman be stationed "near such places" to take the names of all the men entering the business.

The collapse of the great boom in 1888 eased the workload of San Diego's lawmen. As the economic bubble lost air, thousands of people left town. Declining finances forced the council to reduce the police force to fifteen men.

Political change came in March 1889, with voter approval of San Diego's first "modern" city charter. The new charter replaced the old marshal system with a municipal police department of twelve officers. No longer directed by city trustees or councilmen, the department began a new era under Joe Coyne as the city's first chief of police.

THE PEOPLE V. BREEDLOVE

It is not at this writing recalled that any infraction of the peace within the memory of the oldest resident of the community, ever aroused all the people to such white heat and almost explosive indignation as the inexcusable outrage perpetrated by some inflated deputy United States marshals yesterday, in clubbing to death one and beating into insensibility four others of the crew of the United States cruiser Charleston.
—editorial, San Diego Union, *July 15, 1891*

It was a crime that incensed San Diegans—the "murder" of a young sailor from a U.S. warship by a deputized marshal. For one summer and fall, San Diegans would eagerly follow the case of a "posse" gone wild and accused of brutalizing American sailors.

The navy cruiser USS *Charleston* entered San Diego harbor on July 7, 1891. Its sailors, granted liberty after weeks at sea, eagerly headed for the Stingaree, the city's notorious red-light district. Not surprisingly, a few of the seamen were reluctant to return to ship.

It was a common problem, to be dealt with in a time-honored way. A ship's officers would offer a reward of ten dollars for the safe return of each AWOL man. The money would be deducted from the sailor's pay, and he would be denied new shore leave for the next ninety days. Capturing deserters had become a lucrative business for eager San Diego bounty hunters.

When seven of the *Charleston's* crew failed to return to the ship, on July 14, a deputized U.S. marshal, Charles W. Breedlove, and a burly ex-policeman named W.W. Webb armed themselves with "thick set clubs and a six-shooter" and headed for the Stingaree. Breedlove and Webb found four of the sailors in a Fifth Street saloon and attempted to shepherd the men back to the *Charleston*. The sailors ignored the bounty hunters and headed to the ship on their own.

The next morning, the deputized marshals tried again, grabbing two sailors in another Fifth Street bar. This time the blue jackets resisted, and a "lively fight" erupted when a half dozen sailors came running to defend their shipmates. Breedlove and Webb retreated uptown to look for reinforcements.

They returned with a posse of five additional men—all recruited in a local saloon for the promise of $2.50 each for an hour's worth of work. Ten sailors were waiting for them in the street. As scores of bystanders looked on from the sidewalks, the deputies raised their billy clubs and charged. A newspaper reporter described the thirty-minute mêlée that followed:

> *The air was full of clubs and it was first the officers and then the sailors and vice versa, until the combatants mutually separated from exhaustion. The sailors captured the majority of the officers' clubs, several pairs of handcuffs and, it is said, one or two revolvers. They retired to the Silver Moon saloon, at the corner of 3rd and I streets, and entrenched themselves in the second story, where they took stock of their wounds.*

Holding the field of battle, the sailors claimed victory. But they were badly bruised, and some were missing. One of the lost sailors was a twenty-four-year-old fireman from Vallejo named Joseph Brown. A shipmate remembered: "The last time I saw him alive he was staggering down the street. I said, 'How is it Joey?' He replied, 'Oh, they've fixed me Ned; I'm done for.'"

Brown stumbled down the street and collapsed in a horse stable of the Kansas Livery at Fourth and I Streets. The manager of the stables, F.C. McGuire, assumed Brown was intoxicated and laid him down in a grain bin to sleep it off. At 2:00 a.m., a stable boy found the sailor snoring. At 2:45 a.m, the boy reported to McGuire, "He's a layin' awful still, back there."

McGuire checked on Brown and found him dead. The coroner's office was immediately notified. After a cursory examination, Dr. Daniel B. Northrup decided Brown had suspicious abrasions on his scalp and directed that the body be removed for a postmortem.

The next morning, the *San Diego Union* announced in banner headlines, "Clubbed to Death, A Bloody Encounter in Stingaree Town." In fifty-four column inches on the front page, the newspaper reported the story of the deputies' battle with the "unoffending members of the *Charleston*'s crew."

San Diego's county courthouse, built in 1890. *Courtesy of Special Collections, San Diego Public Library.*

The community was outraged. Breedlove and his posse were quickly housed in the county jail and guarded by twenty armed men. *Charleston* sailors vowed to "hang Breedlove and allow his bones to bleach in the sunlight."

A coroner's inquest jury convened at the county's new courthouse on Front and D Streets (Broadway) and took testimony from witnesses for the next three days. Hundreds of onlookers crammed the courtroom, halls and stairways to follow the proceedings. "The most extraordinarily dramatic inquest ever held in the county" rendered its verdict on Friday evening, July 17, deciding that Joseph R. Brown "came to his death as a result of a fracture of the skull caused by a blow from a club known as a Policeman's Billy in the hands of C.W. Breedlove."

The following day, Breedlove and his fellow deputies were charged with murder and assault with a deadly weapon. All except Breedlove quickly made bail. The posse's leader languished in jail until early August, when friends gathered sufficient bond money to release him. The day after his discharge, a man armed with a six-shooter called at Breedlove's home, offering to give the accused a change of venue to "a warmer climate." Fortunately for Breedlove, he had decided to lay low at the home of a friend.

The trial of Charles Breedlove for the murder of Joseph Brown began in September and lingered into the fall. He was found guilty of manslaughter on October 9, 1891. Another indicted deputy, Charles Wilson, was acquitted. Assault charges against the other deputies had already been dismissed.

A bizarre ending awaited Breedlove. Released on bail pending an appeal to the state Supreme Court, he made a trip to Baja California with his father and a friend. Returning to San Diego in July, the three men apparently ran out of water in the desert, and all died of thirst and exposure.

TILL BURNES'S SALOON

A man named Wilbur, who had been a deputy constable under Rice, had part of his nose bitten off yesterday morning by the bear, the property of Till A. Burns. He was in front of the animal's cage at the time, allowing it to lick his face, when the brute relieved him of a part of his nasal protuberance.
—San Diego Union, *April 27, 1886*

Till Burnes and his bear frequently made news in San Diego of the late 1800s. Burnes's sidewalk "menagerie" and his frequent scrapes with the law made the Fifth Street saloonkeeper a memorable pioneer San Diegan.

A native of Arkansas, Tillman A. Burnes came west with his family in 1853 in a wagon train over the Oregon Trail. It was a grim journey for Till, age six. His four-year-old sister, Susan, fell from a wagon and was run over and killed. She was buried at Fort Kearny, Nebraska, and the family traveled on to Portland, Oregon.

After a year in Portland, the Burnes family moved to San Francisco, where young Till learned the engraving business. By age nineteen, he owned his own print shop. But his health failed, and when the family doctor recommended a change in climate, Burnes took a steamship south to investigate San Diego. He stayed a year before returning to San Francisco. Ill health struck again, and Burnes returned to San Diego, this time bringing his wife, Mary.

On January 13, 1875, a newspaper advertisement in the *Union* announced the opening of Till Burnes's Phoenix Saloon—"best wines, liquors and cigars"—at the corner of Fifth and K Streets. For the next thirty years, Till Burnes would be a popular fixture in downtown San Diego.

Burnes's fascination with animals appeared about this time. A centennial celebration in San Diego in July 1876 featured a parade down Fifth Street. "Mr. Till A. Burnes' menagerie," noted the *Union*, "was a uniquely arranged affair, with the numerous singular animals chained on a platform [on his wagon]; it attracted much attention."

Till Burnes standing in front of his Acme Saloon at 500 Fifth Street. The site exists today as a popular Thai restaurant. *Courtesy of the family of Christina Burnes Crosthwaite, granddaughter of Till Burnes.*

Burnes's zoo animals resided on the sidewalk in front of his saloon, but there were occasional runaways. "Till Burns' [*sic*] bear created another sensation yesterday evening," reported the *Union* on August 6, 1881. "It appears that the restive quadruped broke his chain, and went wandering… it was finally determined to 'lass' him, which was accomplished after several 'hairbreadth 'scapes.'" Several people were bitten before the bear was secured by chain to a post.

After the bear made another race for liberty up Fifth Street, Burnes confined the animal to a large cage—"a decidedly much safer way of keeping bruin within bounds," a reporter concluded. "The bear is essentially a vicious animal and to be made perfectly safe must be kept in such a place as to be unable to do damage to passers-by." But confining Burnes's pet did not stop the drunken "man named Wilbur" from losing his nose to the bear in 1886.

Burnes had safer luck with the rest of his caged pets, which included, at various times: a coyote, several monkeys, a vampire bat, a Gila monster and assorted rabbits, pigeons, quail and mockingbirds. Occasionally, the newspapers would mourn the passing of a favorite animal: "The baby leopard seal at Till Burnes' menagerie 'gave up the ghost' on Thursday afternoon. The little fellow took cold during the rain, and it is supposed that it died of quick consumption. Its demise has thrown a gloom over the lower end of Fifth Street."

In 1883, Burnes moved his bar and menagerie to the White House, his new saloon on Fifth Street. As always, Burnes advertised the "Finest Brands of Liquors and Cigars," adding, the "new Monarch Billiard Table...make it the Most Attractive Saloon in town."

Burnes apparently had modest political ambitions. He ran for town constable in 1875 and 1879 but won neither time. He did serve as a volunteer fireman, acting as foreman of San Diego Engine Company No. 1. And for many years, Burnes operated a stage line, running four-horse coaches to El Cajon and Baja California.

Despite his interest in constable work, Burnes had several run-ins with the law. In 1888, he was indicted by the grand jury for allowing gambling in his saloon. Burnes responded by leaving town for an extended vacation. After several weeks of "basking in the sunshine and fatting on the cocoanut milk of Hawaii," he returned to San Diego, where a superior court judge dismissed the charges on a technicality.

Burnes had less success with a judge three years later, when he was convicted of selling drinks in his bar without paying the city's $25-a-month license fee. Years of ignoring the "saloon tax" cost Burnes a fine of $360.

But his biggest scrape occurred in 1881 in a bar shooting the *Union* announced with the headline "Bloody Affray—Two Men Mortally Shot." Headed home after closing his saloon at 4:00 a.m., Burnes stopped at a saloon on the next block to play his guitar at the invitation of the proprietor. Three men entered the bar and began drinking and then fighting. The stocky, five-foot, six-inch Burnes physically separated the drunken combatants and chased them from the saloon. Minutes later, one of the men—a man named Phillips—charged through the door firing a gun. Burnes pulled his own gun—a "self-cocking English bull-dog of the largest calibre"—and returned the fire. Two men were shot: Phillips and a hapless customer named Pedro Verdal.

The Acme Saloon at Fifth and I Streets. *Courtesy of the family of Christina Burnes Crosthwaite, granddaughter of Till Burnes.*

Burnes returned to his own saloon and waited for the constable. Fortunately, both Phillips and Verdal survived their wounds. Burnes was never charged with a crime.

The White House Saloon continued to prosper, but eventually Burnes changed the name to the Acme. His son Tillman Jr. worked as a bartender. The Burnes home, where Till and his wife Mary raised their son and a daughter, Maude, was at Seventh and B Streets. On January 1, 1905, the *Union* announced the passing of "an old landmark." Three months after the death of his wife, Till Burns died of "apoplexy" at age fifty-seven.

RAID ON THE RED-LIGHT DISTRICT

Strolling down Fifth Street any evening, the ear is rasped by the notes from asthmatic pianos, discordant banjos and fiddles, and half-drunken voices that sing boisterous and ribald songs. The eye is pained to see one, two, or perhaps three men on each corner, so intoxicated that they can barely stand…the lower Fifth Street in San Diego is fully as bad, if not worse than the notorious "Barbary Coast" district of San Francisco.
—San Diego Union, *November 3, 1887*

Every city seemed to have one—a seamy section of downtown known as the red-light district. From the boom of the eighties to the early 1900s, San Diego's red lights could be found in the Stingaree, a shabby triangle of city blocks bordered by H Street (now Market Street), Sixth Street and San Diego Bay.

The *San Diego Union* announced the raid on the notorious Stingaree district on November 11, 1912. *Courtesy of Special Collections, San Diego Public Library.*

Saloons, gambling halls, dope peddling and particularly prostitution all flourished here. The proximity to the waterfront made the Stingaree especially attractive to sailors. The booming traffic in sin—illegal, of course—was wide open and blatant. Police and civic officials were content with a hands-off policy, as long as vice and "women of the lewd order" stayed within bounds below H Street.

But public attitudes toward vice were changing rapidly in the early 1900s. Across the nation, the growing progressive movement was spurring cities to close their red-light districts. Chicago began the trend in 1910, followed quickly by Los Angeles, New York, Philadelphia and others.

In San Diego, a vice-suppression committee, better known as the Purity League, met with city officials on October 1, 1912, and urged the police to "slam the lid on the Stingaree." The reformers were most troubled by the prostitutes, who worked out of boardinghouses and tiny shacks and rooms called "cribs." The cribs, as described by a city health inspector, "resembled stalls…built in a long row facing a compound, with one opening leading to each room from outside. A wash bowl and pitcher served as plumbing," along with a "bed and a chair or two. Water was carried from a lone faucet that stood outside." The women paid fourteen dollars a week for the cribs.

Police Chief Keno Wilson argued that closing the district would only scatter prostitution throughout the city. But the reformers were determined. A World's Fair was coming to San Diego in 1915, and it was time to clean up the town.

At 8:00 a.m. on Sunday, November 10, Chief Wilson and thirty patrolmen surrounded the Stingaree and began arresting the prostitutes. The raid caught 138 women who were brought to police headquarters at 732 Second Street (now Second Avenue). A representative of the Purity League appeared before the assembled women and explained that the arrests would only bring happiness to their lives by helping them reform. The women listened respectfully and asked for breakfast. The police brought coffee and ham sandwiches.

Chief Wilson then interrogated each woman, one at a time. Nearly all were young; few admitted to being older than thirty. Most claimed to be new to San Diego, having arrived in recent months. After questioning, the women were released and told to go home and pack their bags.

On Monday morning, the fallen women presented themselves before the justice of the peace, George Puterbaugh. "Before him, the women were lined up in rows of five or ten. He heard their pleas, fined each $100, and suspended the fine on condition they leave town forthwith and not return."

That afternoon, most of the prostitutes boarded a train at the Santa Fe depot and headed to Los Angeles. One witness noticed that nearly all of them bought round-trip tickets.

The closure of the Stingaree district was greeted with less enthusiasm than the Purity League envisioned. Downtown businesses complained of declining trade. Bars and restaurants closed. The *Union* reported in May 1913 that sailors on U.S. warships were demanding San Francisco as their port for liberty, even though San Diego had once been the most popular liberty port on the West Coast.

And as Chief Wilson predicted, the prostitution did not end. Only days after the big roundup, a newspaper reporter noted the number of streetwalkers was growing. Arrests for prostitution would rise in 1913 and then double the following year.

WINGS OVER SAN DIEGO

AN AIRSHIP OR A LEAD BALLOON?

The wonders of this ship are almost beyond any description. Few people in San Diego realize the wonders that have been accomplished during the last few months in the construction of the Toliver airship... When this ship makes its initial flight in May it will make a showing that will startle the whole world.
—newspaper advertisement for the Toliver Aerial Navigation Company, April 5, 1911

The first decade of the 1900s was the era of aviation invention. In 1903, the Wright brothers flew at Kitty Hawk, North Carolina. Primitive airplanes soon followed. But hydrogen-filled airships, such as Germany's zeppelins, were the vanguard of air travel. In 1909, a zeppelin became the first airship used for passenger transport.

When a fifty-six-year-old inventor named Charles H. Toliver appeared in San Diego in 1910 and announced plans to build a forty-passenger dirigible—better known today as a blimp—the town was excited and ready to participate. Little was known about Toliver, but his local public stock offering in the Toliver Aerial Navigation Company sold readily at $2.50 a share.

Toliver's invention, dubbed the *San Diego*, soon began to emerge from a canyon at Thirty-first and B Streets. The airship was 250 feet long and 48 feet in diameter. The metal skeleton was covered with 5,800 yards of "metalized"

Charles Toliver's airship was constructed in a canyon at Thirty-first and B Streets. *Courtesy of San Diego Air & Space Museum.*

silk. Power came from four gasoline engines—thirty-two horsepower each—which Toliver claimed would drive the airship at up to sixty-five miles per hour. Passengers would ride in comfortable safety in a cabin built within the giant gas envelope.

The public seemed fascinated. On Saturday, April 8, 1911, "more than three thousand" people visited the "shipyard" and heard Toliver proclaim his dirigible more than 90 percent complete. The inventor also announced that stock in his company was in such great demand that the share price would now double, to five dollars a share.

Despite assurances of imminent completion, the construction of the blimp, now renamed *Toliver I*, dragged on through the summer of 1911 and into the fall. On October 14, Toliver promised in a public meeting at the U.S. Grant Hotel that the airship would fly within weeks.

On November 10, a throng of excited spectators, and more than a few nervous investors, gathered at the Golden Hill construction site to watch the airship take to the skies. The gas-powered engines started, and the aluminum propellers spun. The *Union* would report: "It quivered for a few breathless moments, threatening to rise, then settled down again."

The harried inventor blamed the weather. A warmer day would have given the ship added buoyancy, he argued. Then he decided that there was

Airship inventor Charles H. Toliver. *Courtesy of San Diego Air & Space Museum.*

too much air in the gas mixture and not enough hydrogen. Bad gas, it seems, had stopped the maiden flight.

But soon Toliver was facing other issues. Some investors complained that their shares of stock were unmarketable. One shareholder filed a lawsuit, alleging problems with Toliver's bookkeeping.

The City Health Department added to Toliver's woes when it announced that the remaining hydrogen in the airship had become "highly explosive and exceedingly dangerous" to the community. Toliver was ordered to "abate the nuisance" by deflating his airship "forthwith."

A winter storm did the job for him. On Wednesday night, December 20, high winds ripped *Toliver I* to shreds, leaving a "formless mass of wreckage." Toliver took the disaster badly, remarking to a newspaper reporter, "The treatment that has been accorded me in San Diego has been unjust and cruel. This may not be the end of the destruction of that airship. Certainly the city officials have been responsible for it and certainly there should be some redress."

One more strange chapter remained in the saga of C.H. Toliver. A former secretary and chauffeur to Toliver, thirty-two-year-old Herbert G. Lewis, was a disgruntled stock investor in Toliver's company. More significantly, Lewis believed his wife, Ellen, had been molested by Toliver.

On Saturday evening, May 25, Lewis was waiting at the Toliver house when the inventor and his wife, Kate, returned home. As the Tolivers drove into the garage, Lewis emerged from the shadows with a gun and shot the couple. Mrs. Toliver staggered into the house and died with the telephone in her hand. Toliver, badly wounded, followed his wife, but as he fell to the floor, Lewis killed him with a butcher knife.

"I guess you've got the man you want," admitted Lewis after the police captured him. "He ruined my home; if I had not done it someone else would have had to."

The case went to trial in February 1913. The jury returned a verdict of "not guilty by reason of insanity." Another jury then deliberated and decided Lewis was now sane. Set free by the court, Lewis and his wife departed for Los Angeles and faded into obscurity.

CHARLES LINDBERGH TAKES FLIGHT

The thrilling and fascinating spectacle of a San Diego–built plane, piloted by a famous army and air mail aviator, racing across the Atlantic Ocean… will be witnessed this summer. A contract for the construction of a monoplane for his proposed New York to Paris non-stop flight was awarded to the Ryan Aircraft Company of this city yesterday by Capt. Charles A. Lindbergh.
—San Diego Union, *March 1, 1927*

In the spring of 1927, several teams of flyers competed for the most celebrated achievement in aviation: the first nonstop, transatlantic crossing. The prestige of such an accomplishment would be accompanied by a cash purse of $25,000, offered by New York hotel owner Raymond Orteig for a flight between New York and Paris. With one exception, all challengers for the "Orteig Prize" featured well-financed teams of two or more airmen in large, multi-engine planes.

The exception was a quietly ambitious mail pilot from the Midwest, Charles Lindbergh. With limited financial backing from bankers in St. Louis and his own meager savings, Lindbergh shopped for an airplane capable of transoceanic flight. He decided to investigate a little-known company from San Diego—Ryan Airlines, which pledged that it could build a custom plane for him in sixty days.

Lindbergh came to San Diego in February 1927. He found the Ryan factory in "an old, dilapidated building" on the waterfront at the foot of Juniper Street. It was a no-frills operation, but Lindbergh was immediately impressed by the enthusiasm of Ryan's owner, B. Franklin Mahoney, and the evident ability of the chief engineer, Donald Hall. "This company is a fit partner," Lindbergh decided. "They're as anxious to build a plane that will fly to Paris as I am to fly it there."

Charles Lindbergh standing alongside his *Spirit of St. Louis*. *Courtesy of San Diego Air & Space Museum.*

With a contract signed for a $10,580 custom-built plane, Lindbergh sat down with Donald Hall to design the single-engine monoplane. His decision to fly solo surprised Hall, who wondered about a navigator and relief pilot. But Lindbergh had decided he would "rather have extra gasoline than an extra man."

Hall was also taken aback by Lindbergh's insistence that the cockpit be placed behind the fuselage gas tank, which meant the pilot had no forward vision. But Lindbergh did not want to be sandwiched between the tank and the engine—a recipe for disaster if the plane crashed. For the flight, Lindbergh would use side windows for sight, along with a periscope mounted on the instrument panel.

To determine the amount of fuel the plane would need, Lindbergh and Hall drove to the San Diego Public Library at 820 E Street. Using a globe and a piece of string, Lindberg estimated the distance from New York to Paris. It came out to 3,600 statute miles, which Hall calculated would require four hundred gallons of gas.

With plans in hand, the Ryan team of thirty-five employees went to work—seven days a week and often into the night. Lindbergh himself worked long hours at the factory, carefully watching the progress and making suggestions based on his flying experience.

As the construction progressed, he spent time at the public library, working out the calculations he would need to conserve fuel and navigate across the Atlantic. The head of the reference section, Grace Arlington Owen, remembered the "tall, young man whose fair hair rose up in unruly fashion." Lindbergh would come in each evening "and remain until near closing time lost in some problem of mathematics."

Lindbergh's San Diego residence in this period is a mystery. His latest biographer, A. Scott Berg (*Lindbergh*, 1998), discovered Lindbergh lived for a time at the U.S. Grant Hotel but then moved to less expensive quarters at the YMCA. Some biographers have claimed he shared an apartment with the Ryan sales manager, A.J. Edwards. Still another candidate for "Charles Lindbergh slept here" is the Palomar Apartments on Sixth Avenue, where Ryan owner B.F. Mahoney lived.

Lindbergh's contract with Ryan had promised a plane in sixty days. The builders finished the work exactly on schedule. The *Spirit of St. Louis*, named in honor of Lindbergh's St. Louis partners, was towed to the Ryan airfield at Dutch Flats, near Barnett Avenue. On April 28, Lindbergh tested the plane for the first time. He later wrote, "I never felt a plane accelerate so fast.

Wings over San Diego

As he prepares to fly from San Diego, Charles Lindbergh is congratulated by pilot Ira Eaker, while Don Hall and A.J. Edwards look on. *Courtesy of San Diego Air & Space Museum.*

Flying solo across the Atlantic with a single engine was an enormous risk. The plane's builders had their doubts. "We were skeptical ourselves," recalled machinist Ed Morrow, "that even our plane would be able to make it."

Along with possible engine failure, Lindbergh's greatest fear was falling asleep. New York to Paris would require over thirty hours of flying. The pilot had to stay alert the entire time—not just flying the plane but monitoring gas consumption and navigating with minimal instruments. In preparing for the flight, many witnesses in San Diego would later say Lindbergh trained to stay awake by walking for hours at night—a claim dismissed by biographer Berg as myth.

Lindbergh made twenty-three training flights in the *Spirit of St. Louis* in ten days. The plane performed flawlessly. On May 10, Lindbergh prepared to leave Dutch Flats for a short hop to North Island before departing for the East Coast. He thanked the employees of Ryan for their "grand" work and, saying goodbye to Ed Morrow, remarked, "Well, Ed, I guess this is goodbye—I might get wet." Morrow assured him that wouldn't happen; their plane "was built to fly the Atlantic."

Late that afternoon, Lindbergh took off from North Island for a night flight to St. Louis. Lindbergh had never flown all night before, but he needed to test his plane and navigation skills in darkness. He reached St. Louis in record time and then departed for New York the following day.

At Roosevelt Field on Long Island, Lindbergh waited for rainy weather to clear. He finally lifted the *Spirit of St. Louis* off a muddy runway on

Friday morning, May 20. Thirty-three and a half hours later, Lindbergh landed at Le Bourget Field, Paris—the first person to fly nonstop across the Atlantic Ocean.

RUTH ALEXANDER: PIONEER OF THE AIR

An unconscious girl slumped in the cockpit of a tiny monoplane as it soared five miles above Lindbergh Field was believed today to have achieved a new altitude record for women.
—Associated Press, July 12, 1930

New feats in aviation were treasured news stories in the early twentieth century. In San Diego, the self-proclaimed "Air Capitol of the West," aviation heroes were followed eagerly—few more closely than a young aviator named Ruth Alexander.

Born in Irving, Kansas, in 1905, Ruth Blaney Alexander was the only child of a hardware store dealer and a schoolteacher. She grew up playing with tools, building kites and dreaming of flying. At age seven, she shocked her mother one day by jumping from the top of a barn, holding an umbrella as a parachute. The experiment failed, but Ruth was unhurt.

She got her first chance to fly when she was twenty. A barnstorming plane touched down in a hay field near her town on the Fourth of July. After a short five-dollar flight in a "baling wire wonder," Ruth was determined to pursue a career as an aviator.

Four years later, with money saved from working in a beauty parlor in Olathe, Kansas, she abandoned a brief marriage to one Mac Alexander and headed for California, hitching a ride with a family that needed help driving the car. Five days later, she ended up in Coronado. Living in a rented room, Alexander found a job as a beautician and worked nights at a soda fountain in San Diego.

She entered a "Queen of the Air" contest that offered flying lessons sponsored by the *San Diego Sun*. She failed to win but still caught the eye of Earl Prudden of the Ryan School of Aviation. Prudden recognized rare talent in the twenty-four-year-old girl and offered her a spot in his flying school.

On September 9, 1929, Alexander began Prudden's twenty-lesson course in flying. Recording the experience in her diary, she wrote: "Whee! I was in the air today. Don't know whether I was alright or not but I was happy. I know I'll be able to learn."

Ruth Alexander sits on the cockpit of her Barling monoplane. *Courtesy of San Diego Air & Space Museum.*

Alexander learned quickly and soloed for the first time on October 25. Earning her pilot's license only weeks later, she became the sixty-fifth licensed female pilot in the United States. She celebrated her new credential by flying a ninety-horsepower Great Lakes biplane to 15,500 feet over San Diego. The altitude was a record height for women in light planes.

"I was all over the newspapers," Alexander recalled. "People looked at me like I was something in a zoo." Surprised executives at the Great Lakes Company of Cleveland, Ohio, sent the rising star a check for $100.

Her days were spent flying whenever the weather was good. "Happier and happier as I learn more and more," she recorded in her diary. "I love acrobatics, my Russell parachute seems good to me each time I start a spin."

Determined to set more records but still struggling financially, she moved into a room at the Maryland Hotel on F Street to be closer to the airfield. And she got financial backing for a new plane: a low-winged, Barling monoplane.

On July 4, 1930—exactly fifteen years after her first experience in the air—she attempted to break her own altitude record. Several hundred spectators at Lindbergh Field squinted skyward as Alexander circled above in her monoplane. When her altimeter reached twenty thousand feet, the needle froze. After flying for two hours, the aviator landed, believing she had topped twenty-one thousand feet.

One week later, she tried again, this time carrying a sealed barograph in addition to her altimeter. Dressed warmly for the open cockpit and breathing oxygen from a tube, Alexander soared above her old record, but as she rose above twenty-six thousand feet, her oxygen failed and she passed out, apparently for several minutes. When she regained consciousness, the plane was at eighteen thousand feet "in a gentle left bank, slowly settling."

"It didn't feel so good, without any oxygen," she told reporters later, "so I dove down to about 7000 feet, and then came down more slowly." The sealed barograph—forwarded that night by air mail to the National Aeronautical Association in Washington, D.C.—would show 26,600 feet, a new light plane record for both men and women.

The feat made national news, with the near-disastrous oxygen failure providing the headlines. "UNCONSCIOUS GIRL RISES 26,000 FEET" read the Washington, D.C. *Evening Star*. "SETS ALTITUDE MARK BUT LOSES HER SENSES" headlined the *New York Times*.

With sponsorship from the Agua Caliente resort in Tijuana, Ruth Alexander was the first female aviator to traverse the Pacific coast of the United States without touching ground. *Courtesy of San Diego Air & Space Museum.*

For her next exploit, Alexander secured sponsorship from the Agua Caliente Resort in Tijuana to attempt a three-country flight along the Pacific coast. On August 28, Alexander set off from Vancouver, British Columbia, and headed south. Burning 117 gallons of fuel, she averaged ninety-one miles per hour on her sixteen-hour, nonstop trip. When Alexander landed at Agua Caliente, she was the first female aviator to traverse the Pacific coast of the United States without touching it.

A one-stop flight to the East Coast was next on Alexander's agenda. Now with a national following, financial backing had become easier. She planned to fly to historic Roosevelt Field, Long Island—the site of Lindbergh's transatlantic start—with only a stop in Wichita, Kansas, en route.

Alexander took off from Lindbergh Field at 3:28 a.m. on September 18. Once again carrying a heavy fuel load of 117 gallons, the plane climbed slowly and disappeared in heavy fog. Friends had warned her not to bank the plane east until it gained altitude. "I know," she replied, "and I won't do it."

Only minutes later, Alexander crashed on a hillside in Point Loma. The remains of the plane were scattered over four hundred feet in Plumosa Park. The body of Ruth Alexander was found pinned among mangled braces and struts of the twisted fuselage.

National headlines carried the news of the tragedy. But the exact cause of the accident would be a mystery. Officially, San Diego's Board of Air Control decided the "heavily, overloaded" plane had fallen into a spin and struck the ground in a vertical position "with the motor full on."

America's First Airline

In war surplus biplanes, aviation pioneers T. Claude Ryan and B. Franklin Mahoney made history on March 1, 1925. The launch of their Los Angeles–San Diego Air Line would be America's first regularly scheduled, daily airline service.

The Ryan Flying Company, based at the airfield of Dutch Flats, north of today's Marine Corp. Recruit Depot, had been profitable for Claude Ryan. The veteran flyer piloted many of his firm's charter and sightseeing excursions. His trips to and from Los Angeles were particularly lucrative. In 1924, friend and future business partner B.F. Mahoney suggested expanding the L.A. run into an airline service with a daily, year-round schedule. Mahoney offered to underwrite expenses for the operation, and Ryan would fly the planes.

The gamble seemed worth it. Ryan bought three Standard J-1 planes in Texas for a few hundred dollars each and had the disassembled planes—last used as army trainers in World War I—shipped to San Diego. Unimpressed by his own purchase, Ryan noted that the planes "had no engines and were really just a batch of parts."

His mechanics added single engines and quickly put the planes into flying shape. In the forward cockpit, they created an enclosed space for four passengers. Side windows provided a view for each traveler. The pilot flew the plane from a rear cockpit left open to the sky. In temperate Southern California, Ryan was unconcerned about his wiper-less windshield: "When it rained I'd just stand up in the cockpit and look over the windshield. At 80 mph and 100 feet of altitude we could get along okay."

One of Ryan's biplanes—larger than the other two—boasted a side-by-side rear cockpit that could seat an extra co-pilot or mechanic. This plane, the designated "flagship" of the airline fleet, was christened the *Palomar*, the name of the building at Sixth and Maple where Ryan and Mahoney had apartments.

Claude Ryan in the cockpit of a Ryan Standard with his sisters Louise (rear) and Kathryn. *Courtesy of San Diego Air & Space Museum.*

(Three years later, Charles Lindbergh would purportedly bunk at the Palomar Apartments as he supervised the construction of the *Spirit of St. Louis*.)

Ryan decided on a fare of $22.50 for a round-trip ticket. He had already calculated that amount as the break-even cost for each flight (even with only one passenger). A one-way fare was $14.50, hotel transportation included.

On Sunday morning, March 1, the airline was ready to debut. Shrewdly, Ryan and Mahoney recruited Hollywood celebrities as their first passengers. Thousands of sightseers and movie fans converged on the airfield at Ninety-ninth Street and Western Avenue in Los Angeles to see the celebrities and witness the inaugural flight. One hour before departure, a dozen movie stars, including director Robert Vignola, actress Hedda Hopper and Cecil B. DeMille star Vera Reynolds, lined up for photographers while police pushed back the crowds.

Airplanes from the U.S. Army and Navy would escort the "huge cabin passenger planes" to San Diego. Thirty minutes before takeoff, three military planes swooped over the airfield and "hovered about in the air until the signal to point south was given."

Departure came at 10:00 a.m. Flying at 1,500 feet—with Claude Ryan piloting one of the celebrity planes himself—the flight south took ninety minutes. Two navy carrier pigeons were released as the three Ryan "airliners"

Hollywood celebrities crowded around the Ryan airliner on the first day of operations. *Courtesy of San Diego Air & Space Museum.*

took off; one of the pigeons would reach its North Island perch before the planes landed in San Diego.

At the Dutch Flats, a huge crowd was waiting as the six planes—flying in perfect formation—touched down on the dirt landing strip. Cameramen from the San Diego Cinema Corp. cranked film footage of the stars as they disembarked and were greeted by the mayor and members of the chamber of commerce "aviation committee." Lunch at the U.S. Grant Hotel came next, followed by several rounds of congratulatory speeches. The movie stars were given an afternoon tour of the city and then whisked back to the airfield for a return flight to Los Angeles.

The *San Diego Union* praised the new project and predicted it would "set a precedent for civil aircraft development." The next day, the airline began its scheduled service: daily flights between San Diego and Los Angeles, with departures from the north at 9:00 a.m. and returns at 4:00 p.m.

Profits, however, were disappointing. As the novelty of the airline route declined, so did passenger traffic. To boost income, fares were raised to $17.40 one way and $26.50 round trip. But most Ryan revenue continued to come from charter and sightseeing flights.

To stimulate interest, the fledgling airline purchased a larger plane built by Donald Douglas, of future DC airliner fame. With a wingspan of fifty-six feet and a length of thirty-seven feet, the *Cloudster* biplane dwarfed the three Ryan Standards. The open-cockpit fuselage was enclosed to accommodate ten passengers in a plush cabin with padded seats, carpeting, overhead dome lights and ash trays.

But the well-appointed airliner did little to boost profits. Ryan and Mahoney kept their daily schedule as long as they could—sometimes flying empty planes between cities. Eventually, they chose to concentrate on airplane manufacturing. After less than two years of operation, the pioneering Los Angeles–San Diego Air Line closed operations.

A Sporting City

Seabiscuit v. Ligaroti

That was as rough a race as I've ever seen in my whole life. They were hitting each other over the head with their whips and Richardson had Woolf in a leg-lock. Never seen so much trouble in one race and there was a hell of a stink about it.
—Oscar Otis, track announcer, August 12, 1938

It was the event that put the Del Mar racetrack on the map. The horse racing duel between the thoroughbreds Seabiscuit and Ligaroti drew more than twenty thousand fans to the seaside track, while a captivated nationwide audience listened to the race on a live radio broadcast.

In only its second season, the Del Mar racetrack needed a spark to boost sagging attendance. Bing Crosby's $600,000 investment was attracting only about 5,000 fans each race day—drawn largely from San Diego's quiet population of fewer than 200,000 or from Los Angeles, one hundred miles away by train. But a match race between California's biggest sports celebrity—Seabiscuit—and Ligaroti, a rising star from Argentina, promised national exposure and a big gate.

A friendly family rivalry led to the famous race. Lin Howard, who owned Ligaroti along with Bing Crosby, was the son of Charles S. Howard, owner of Seabiscuit. The two horses had faced each other before. Seabiscuit had won, but Ligaroti was improving fast, winning three of his last four starts. Lin Howard thought his horse was ready to upset the 'Biscuit and challenged his father to a head-to-head race. The two Howards struck a deal to run a mile and one-eighth on August 12. It would be an exhibition race with no public betting. But the owners would compete for a purse of $25,000, winner take all.

A poster promoting the race listed the matchups: Father v. Son, Charles Howard v. Bing Crosby, America v. Argentina. Even the trainers were matched up: Seabiscuit's trainer was "Silent Tom" Smith, while Ligaroti was trained by Smith's son, Jimmy.

A record crowd filled the grandstand on the day of the race. Lin Howard set up a cheering section for Ligaroti. His designated cheerleader was David Butler, director of several Shirley Temple movies and later the *Leave It to Beaver* TV series. Butler wore a red sweater emblazoned with a big "BL" for Binglin, the name for the Crosby and Howard stable. Hundreds of rooters waved pennants with small Ls for Ligaroti. Bing Crosby and actor

Trainer Tom Smith leads Seabiscuit from a railroad car before the great race at Del Mar. *Courtesy of Del Mar Thoroughbred Club.*

Headed for the finish, Seabiscuit led Ligaroti by a nose as the two jockeys fought each other.
Courtesy of Del Mar Thoroughbred Club.

Pat O'Brien watched from the roof of the grandstand, behind a microphone that would call the race for the radio audience.

"Seabiscuit by one punch" was the consensus prediction. But the *San Diego Sun* boldly predicted the favorite would win by eight lengths, "unless he is pulled up to give Ligaroti a chance." To even the odds, both owners had agreed to a big weight advantage for the underdog: Ligaroti would run with 115 pounds, Seabiscuit would carry 130.

A coin toss determined the starting position, and Seabiscuit won the important inside post. Trainer Tom Smith told his jockey, George "The Iceman" Woolf, to go for the early lead and get clear of Ligaroti.

Both horses broke cleanly from the gate. Seabiscuit led by a half length going into the first turn. Aboard Ligaroti, jockey Noel "Spec" Richardson drew within a head of Seabiscuit and stayed there. Going into the final turn, the horses were matched stride for stride, close to the rail, only inches apart.

The crowd was frantic. So were the jockeys. Unable to pass Seabiscuit, Spec Richardson reached over and grabbed Woolf's saddlecloth. Woolf

A glum Bing Crosby watches as Seabiscuit owner Charles Howard accepts the winner's trophy. *Courtesy of Del Mar Thoroughbred Club.*

fought back with his whip. Then Richardson locked his leg with Woolf's. As the horses approached the wire, a desperate Woolf grabbed Ligaroti's bridle and tugged. They crossed the finish line with Seabiscuit ahead by a nose.

The victory set a new track record (1:49) that smashed the old mark by four seconds. The crowd was thrilled but was surprised when the inquiry sign flashed almost immediately. The two jockeys stormed off the track, both claiming the other had fouled. Bing Crosby met the riders in the jockeys' room and told them to keep quiet.

After a brief consultation, the track stewards declared Seabiscuit the official winner. Woolf and Richardson, however, were suspended.

Days later, the Del Mar stewards watched grainy film footage of the jockey duel down the home stretch. While it seemed to show Richardson as the aggressor, the stewards decided to lift the suspensions on both riders since the race had been an exhibition with no public betting involved.

The exciting race stayed in the public's attention for days. Then the *Sun* added a new controversy with the claim that Seabiscuit's rider, George Woolf, had been instructed "to hold his horse in" and "make a race out of

116

it." It was further alleged that Richardson, knowing of Woolf's orders, had placed large bets on Ligaroti.

Charles Howard dismissed the charge, saying, "It would be foolish to give a jockey aboard Seabiscuit orders to make it close because Seabiscuit has a tendency to loaf if he's ahead." Howard also pointed out that Seabiscuit's record time "proved that he was really running and that Ligaroti is a much better horse than we figured."

Both horses would finish the 1938 season on top. Ligaroti would win the Del Mar Handicap. Seabiscuit, in the best-known race of his storied career, would defeat Triple Crown winner War Admiral on November 1 in another match race. But for Del Mar, the classic duel will always be Seabiscuit v. Ligaroti.

WESTGATE PARK: HOME OF THE PADRES

Not even Yankee Stadium or Boston's Fenway Park can surpass the comforts and conveniences of the Padres' new home…This is a real ballpark, built for the game of baseball, a ballpark in which the city of San Diego can take great pride.
—*Jack Murphy,* San Diego Union, *April 22, 1958*

With great enthusiasm, the *Union's* sports columnist, Jack Murphy, celebrated the wonders of Westgate Park, San Diego's new baseball stadium in Mission Valley. "It's clean, it's modern, it's classic in its simplicity." The million-dollar structure replaced the aged Lane Field, the downtown stadium at Broadway and Harbor Drive, where the Pacific Coast League (PCL) Padres had played since 1936.

Local businessman C. Arnholt Smith, owner of the Westgate-California Tuna Packing Company, had acquired the Padres in 1955. He immediately made plans to replace the "termite village" with a modern stadium to showcase his new property.

Building a minor league ballpark with private capital was risky in 1957. The nation was in a serious recession. PCL officials also worried that the pending moves of the Brooklyn Dodgers and the New York Giants to California would kill interest in local minor league baseball

And the site of Westgate Park—in the "pastoral heartland" of undeveloped Mission Valley—was controversial. Smith won approval for the project only after serious courting of the city council. Ignoring objections by the Planning Commission, which feared growing commercialization in the valley, the council blessed the project in the fall of 1956.

Spacious Westgate Park was built along Friar's Road, the site of today's Fashion Valley Shopping Center. *Courtesy of Bill Swank.*

After a vigorous construction schedule, which included surfacing Friar's Road—the access street from Highway 395 (today's 163)—the stadium was introduced to the public in a "Meet the Padres" open house on April 28, 1958. Free buses ferried fans to the stadium from Horton Plaza. Comedian Joe E. Brown was the featured speaker for the box lunch. The Padre players were introduced, wearing their new, pinstripe white uniforms.

The fans found a stadium with a seating capacity of 8,268—small by Major League standards but spacious for the minor league Padres. There were 5,752 box seats and 2,516 grandstand seats. There were no bleachers, and every theater-style seat featured an armrest. A steel roof shaded almost the entire grandstand.

The concession stands were a wonder. Jack Murphy marveled at the vast kitchen in the "catacombs" under the stands, with its walk-in coolers for beer and soft drinks. He was particularly impressed by the heated storage room (temperature was maintained at 120 degrees) for peanuts, which held ten thousand bags of peanuts, twenty-three peanuts to a bag.

Opening day was Tuesday, April 29: a double-header against the Phoenix Giants, led by twenty-year-old, future Hall of Famer Willie McCovey. The afternoon game drew 4,619 fans who watched their team beat the Giants 5–3, led by strong pitching from Dick Stigman.

A steel roof covered the comfortable grandstand at Westgate. *Courtesy of Bill Swank.*

The night game drew 7,129. Actor Dick Powell threw the opening pitch to Pacific Coast League president Leslie O'Connor. The Giants' McCovey was held in check, but Dusty Rhodes—the New York Giants hero of the 1954 World Series—hit Westgate's first home run. The Padres responded with a homer by Larry Raimes and by the sidearm pitching of Bill Werle. They took the nightcap, 3–1.

Most of the ballplayers of that opening day were in the twilight of their careers. The Padre stars—Rudy Regalado, Bill Werle, Larry Raimes—would soon be out of baseball. Dick Stigman would have several productive years with the Cleveland Indians and Minnesota Twins. Several Giant players of that day—Willie McCovey, Tom Haller, Leon Wagner, Joey Amalfitano—were starting successful Major League careers.

The Padres would play ten years at Westgate Park and win three PCL championships: 1962, 1964 and 1967. Ballpark expansion was contemplated for a time in the mid-1960s when the Milwaukee Braves briefly considered moving west. Blueprints were drawn up to add a second deck and outfield bleachers, bringing the seating capacity to forty thousand.

But instead of expansion, Westgate Park would get a pink slip. In December 1967, plans were announced for a $40 million shopping center to be built on the site of the ballpark by Westgate-California Realty and developer Ernest

The Westgate Padres hold the 1964 championship trophy for the Pacific Coast League. *Clockwise*: pitcher Ray Ripplemeyer, businessman Harry Douglas, manager Dave Bristol, C. Arnholt Smith's daughter Shannon Smith, coach Whitey Wietelmann, pitcher Jim Coates and shortstop Chico Ruiz. *Courtesy of Bill Swank*.

W. Hahn. "The finest minor league facility in the country" fell to a wrecking ball, and the Fashion Valley Mall emerged in its place two years later.

San Diego's PCL Padres opened the 1968 season in the new San Diego Stadium. The same year, the city was awarded a National League franchise. The Padres returned the next year as a Major League team. San Diego Stadium, renamed Jack Murphy in 1980 and then Qualcomm in 1997, hosted the Padres until their move to PETCO Park in 2004.

THE CHARGERS COME TO SAN DIEGO

The Chargers got off the longest quick kick in Civic Center history yesterday, booting themselves right out of apathetic Los Angeles and into eager, enthusiastic San Diego.
—*Jerry Magee, San Diego Union, January 25, 1961*

In the winter of 1961, the San Diego City Council unanimously endorsed professional football in the city. A whirlwind courtship that lasted only weeks brought Barron Hilton's Los Angeles Chargers south. The city's first big league sports team would begin the 1961 football season in Balboa Stadium as the San Diego Chargers.

Jack Murphy, the sports editor of the *Union*, had begun lobbying for the Chargers in a notable column on December 21, 1960: "The story will be denied and I'll probably be denounced as a third-rate fiction writer but it comes on excellent authority that the Los Angeles Charger franchise is San Diego's for the asking."

The Chargers were a new team in a new league. In their first season, they played for the American Football League championship—losing narrowly to the Houston Oilers on New Year's Day 1961. But Los Angeles—home of the well-established NFL Rams—was not interested in the Chargers. Playing in the cavernous, 100,000-seat Coliseum, the Chargers sometimes drew only 10,000 fans.

"There's no doubt in my mind that we've got to get out of Los Angeles," Hilton concluded. "We can't compete in the same market with the Rams. A lot of cities would like to have us...I'd prefer to put the club in San Diego."

But the shrewd businessman, son of hotel magnate Conrad Hilton, made it clear that he had conditions: "If we move to San Diego, we're going to need a lot of help there." The best site for hosting pro football was forty-six-year-old Balboa Stadium. But with a seating capacity of fewer than twenty-four thousand, it would need expansion and a major renovation.

Hilton was willing to lose money at first —he had dropped an estimated $900,000 in Los Angeles—but he wanted a future. In San Diego, there was the promise of lucrative television rights and an excellent chance for joining the National Football League with that league's unannounced but anticipated merger with the AFL.

San Diego's business and civic leaders saw the acquisition of the Chargers as a path to national recognition for the country's eighteenth largest city. Sensitive about its reputation as a mere navy town—"an airport tied to a submarine" is what one sports executive called the city—San Diegans believed pro football would inspire civic pride. It also made good business sense. Hilton's team was a million-dollar company with a player payroll of $385,000. Jack Murphy predicted that every dollar spent by the Chargers would come back seven times.

Charger football was even endorsed by the baseball Padres, who also had Major League aspirations. "The Chargers will be good for baseball," said Padres executive Doug Giddings, "because they will awaken spectator sports in San Diego."

On January 5, 1961, Hilton came to San Diego for a visit with Mayor Charles Dail and other civic leaders. Along with Chargers coach and general manager Sid Gillman, Hilton visited Balboa Stadium to look over the field and locker room. The immediate problem they saw was the stadium's small size. That could be fixed with a reconfigured field and a second tier of seats.

But the locker room was a shock. "A real hell-hole," said Coach Gillman. "I was pretty blue after seeing the place." Cold and dark, it was so small that visiting teams had no lockers and used baskets and coat hangers to hold their clothes.

The Chargers' first exhibition game in 1961 came against the Houston Oilers. Note the unfinished second deck of Balboa Stadium in the background. *Courtesy of Todd Tobias.*

Quarterback Jack Kemp (15) throwing against the Houston Oilers in the 1961 AFL championship game. *Courtesy of Todd Tobias.*

By the end of the visit, Hilton said the Chargers would relocate if the city would renovate the locker room and increase stadium seating to at least thirty thousand. Hilton also wanted a fan base that could provide season ticket sales of twenty thousand.

San Diego was excited. The junior chamber of commerce was swamped with pledges for season tickets. The January 8 sports section of the *Union* bore the headline "Chargers' Drive Rolls!"

The following week, Coach Gillman and a team of engineers, architects and landscapers scoured the stadium to determine exactly what improvements the Chargers would request from the city. "If the club is going to be on television every week Balboa Stadium has got to be made a showplace," said Gillman.

Barron Hilton personally presented the final proposal to the city council on January 24. In the contract negotiations that followed, the city agreed to pay for all the stadium improvements. The $700,000 required would come from city operating funds. With some dissent, the councilmen also approved Hilton's demand for one year of rent-free use of Balboa Stadium, $2,000 rent per game the second year and a fixed rate of 5 percent of the gross thereafter. The five-year contract was signed on February 9.

One week later, the Chargers announced the ticket scale for the 1961 season. Premium sideline seats would go for five dollars, reserve seats outside that area would be three dollars and general admission would be two dollars. Season tickets for seven league games were thirty-five dollars.

Reconstruction of the stadium was quickly underway—aiming for completion by the start of the football season in September. But change orders slowed the work, and costs escalated. When the budget passed $1 million, the city decided to defer several budgeted projects, including fire and police stations, Mission Bay improvements and a branch library in Ocean Beach.

Working around the clock, the expanded stadium was ready for the Chargers' home opener on September 17, when they routed the Oakland Raiders, 44–0. In the next few years—with stars like Jack Kemp, Lance Alworth, Ron Mix and Paul Lowe—the team dominated its division in the AFL. The Chargers moved to the new San Diego Stadium in Mission Valley in 1967 and joined the National Football League in 1970.

A FLOATING STADIUM ON MISSION BAY

The floating stadium would be perfect for San Diego, particularly if it was located in Mission Bay. It's the first novel idea in stadium-building since the dome.
—*Barron Hilton, October 1964*

Hotel magnate and San Diego Chargers owner Barron Hilton was excited. A creative proposal from the local firm Boyle Engineering suggested a new sports stadium for San Diego that would float in the waters of Mission Bay. Hosting football, Major League baseball and aquatic events, the stadium would seat over fifty thousand fans on a site near Fiesta Island.

As planned by the Boyle engineers, the stadium would consist of three huge sections. The center section—a grandstand, seating about thirteen thousand—would be landlocked. Two wings, seating twenty thousand each, would float on pontoons and could be easily maneuvered into various configurations to support the spectator requirements of different sports.

For baseball, the two wings would be attached to the center grandstand. For football, the wings would be disengaged and floated over to cover both

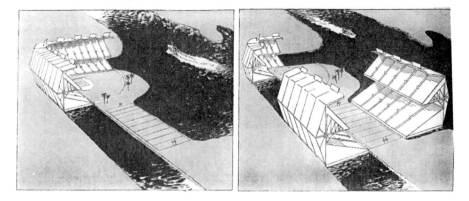

San Diego's proposed "floating stadium" would consist of a landlocked grandstand
with movable wings, which floated on pontoons that could be maneuvered into needed
configurations. San Diego Union, *June 11, 1964.*

sides of a separate playing field. With other configurations, fans could watch
water sports on the bay. Requiring only eleven feet of draft, the sections
would move easily. "As a stunt," one engineer suggested, "we could have
them pulled by circus elephants."

The price tag appeared cheap: an estimated $20 million—about the same
cost as a conventional stadium. It was "the most daring, yet practical concept
in stadium building since Houston discovered the dome," enthused Jack
Murphy, the respected sports columnist for the *San Diego Union.*

San Diego's need for a large, multipurpose sports stadium was critical.
After several years in the cramped quarters of aging Balboa Stadium, the
Chargers were considering a move to Anaheim, and the minor league Padres
were hopeful of a promotion to the big leagues—possible only if San Diego
built a new stadium.

A feasibility study commissioned by the city and county and released in
November 1964 examined several potential sites for the project, dubbed
the All-American Stadium. Westgate Park, the Mission Valley home of the
Padres, was quickly eliminated; the experts from Western Management
Consultants judged the property too expensive to expand. A Kearny Mesa
site appeared more promising, with good highway access and open areas for
a large facility with lots of parking.

The highest marks went to Mission Bay. The site was already city-owned,
so property costs would not be a negative factor. Temperate weather by
the ocean was favorable; after studying long-term weather patterns, the
consultants scoffed at fears of chilly game nights common to San Francisco's
Candlestick Park.

The most impressive feature of the Mission Bay site was the flexibility of the buoyant, multipurpose stadium. The consultants praised the unique use of flotation to move the tiers of seating to accommodate different sports. The location also took advantage of the features of Mission Bay Park, particularly the viewing of major aquatic events such as boat racing.

The San Diego press corps was convinced. Jack Murphy, who had championed the successful Westgate Park in 1958, wrote, "In the long run, the floating stadium would be cheaper to maintain, there's better parking and it would be a bigger tourist attraction than the Houston dome." Barron Hilton made his endorsement clear, declaring the floating stadium "the finest home for a football team that I can imagine."

With sentiment clearly favoring a floating arena in Mission Bay, the city selected the architectural firm Frank L. Hope and Associates to prepare a second feasibility study that would nominate one site for the All-American Stadium. But the new study, released on March 9, 1965, expressed doubts about the popular idea. "Every time we go through the floating concept we find new problems," said architect Frank Hope.

The biggest problem was simply cost. Hope calculated the final price tag of a floating stadium would exceed $41 million—over twice the original estimate. Troublesome expenditures included $7 million for the pontoons needed to move the floating sections and $4 million for foundations. The engineering costs would raise the price to more than $500 per stadium seat. Hope recommended, instead, a fifty-thousand-seat multipurpose facility in Mission Valley that could be built for $300 a seat for a final cost of only $23.5 million.

"It will be a conventional stadium," conceded Jack Murphy, "conventional in the sense it won't float." But the San Diego City Council was reluctant to let go of the stadium on water. "I still think the idea has a lot of merit," said Councilman Jack Walsh. "I wouldn't give up on the floating stadium right away."

Entranced by the uniqueness of the idea, the nationwide publicity the city would garner and the economic spark it could provide for developing Mission Bay, the council unanimously directed Frank Hope to revisit the Mission Bay stadium.

But when Hope reported back five weeks later, the findings were the same. The city could expect "extremely high costs" in several phases of construction. The council unanimously endorsed the Mission Valley stadium on April 28, 1965.

In the fall, San Diego voters approved a $27 million bond measure to build the conventional, multipurpose facility. San Diego Stadium was completed in less than two years, hosting the Chargers in the stadium's first game on August 20, 1967.

SAN DIEGANS TO REMEMBER

THE NEWSPAPERMAN

After surmounting difficulties and suffering anxieties that would have disheartened any but a "live Yankee," we are enabled to present the first number of the Herald *to the public.*
—*John Judson Ames,* San Diego Herald

San Diego's first newspaper, the *Herald*, appeared on May 29, 1851, only twelve days after the first issue of the *Los Angeles Star*—the earliest newspaper in Southern California. The editor and publisher of the *Herald* was thirty-year-old John Judson Ames, a towering, six-foot, six-inch "live Yankee" from Calais, Maine.

Ames had come west with the Gold Rush, arriving in San Francisco in October 1849. He came penniless and began his California career by working for other forty-niners, hauling trunks and luggage with a borrowed handcart. But the ambitious Ames had a literary bent, experience running a newspaper in New Orleans and an interest in politics.

In late 1850, Ames visited San Diego. There were fewer than seven hundred people in the former Mexican pueblo, but prospects for a southern transcontinental railroad seemed hopeful. If San Diego could secure the

John Judson Ames, editor and publisher
of the second-oldest newspaper in
Southern California, the *Herald*.
*Courtesy of Special Collections, San Diego
Public Library.*

railroad before San Francisco or Los Angeles, it would become an important town, perhaps the leading city of California.

Establishing a newspaper in San Diego became Ames's goal. Getting the broadsheet started, however, was a nightmare. The transport of his printing equipment all the way from New Orleans to California across the Isthmus of Panama nearly ended in disaster. Ames explained in his first issue of the *Herald*:

> *We issued our prospectus in December last, and supposed at the time that we had secured the material of our paper; but when we came to put our hand on it, it wasn't there! Determined to lose no time, we took the first boat for New Orleans, where we selected our office, and had returned as far as the Isthmus, when Dame Misfortune gave us another kick, snagged our boat, and sunk everything in the Chagres River.*

The tenacious Ames fished boxes of type and his 1,200-pound press out of the river, fought off an attack of tropical fever and—while waiting three months for a steamship to take him back to California—rebounded by starting the bilingual *Panama Herald*, the first newspaper ever published in Panama.

When Ames finally opened shop in San Diego, he produced a four-page, four-column newspaper, measuring twelve by eighteen inches. Advertisements—typically from San Francisco merchants—filled most of

VOL. 1. SAN DIEGO, CAL., THURSDAY, MAY 29, 1851. NO. 1.

The first issue of the *Herald* appeared on May 29, 1851. *Courtesy of Special Collections, San Diego Public Library.*

the columns, including the entire front page. News and opinion appeared on page two, spilling over to page three. Annual subscriptions cost ten dollars.

"Independent in all things, neutral in nothing" was the Ames editorial motto, but in the next few years, the paper would mostly support Democrats, such as California governor John Bigler (1852–56). But Ames could be a maverick at times. In 1855, the *Herald* suggested Texas hero Sam Houston for president. The next year, Ames endorsed Millard Fillmore of the nativist Know Nothing Party and adopted a new slogan for the *Herald*: "Thoroughly American in principle, sentiment and effort."

Ames's years at the *Herald* were often interrupted by business trips to San Francisco, where he courted advertisers and political contacts. In the summer of 1853, Ames left town to attend Democratic Party business in San Francisco. On the eve of his departure, he announced to his readers: "We shall leave on the steamer for San Francisco, to be absent about two weeks. A friend of acknowledged ability and literary acquirements will occupy the 'old arm chair' during our absence."

The friend was Lieutenant George Horatio Derby, thirty, an army engineer who was stationed in San Diego to lead an engineering project on the San Diego River. Derby was a talented humorist and writer. Under the pseudonym of "John Phoenix," he produced six notable issues of the *Herald*, enlivening the columns with witty commentary and satire.

As editor pro tem, Derby would be remembered throughout California for a prank. Ames had often reminded his readers to vote for the Democratic candidate for governor, John Bigler. But overnight, Derby turned the *Herald*'s politics from Democrat to Whig and encouraged readers to support the Whig candidate, William Waldo. In the election, Waldo would carry San Diego but narrowly lose to Bigler statewide. Ames took the practical joke in stride and announced on his return: "Here we are again! Phoenix has played the 'devil' during our absence, but he has done it in such a good humored manner, that we have not a word to say."

For most of the 1850s, Ames struggled to keep his *Herald* in print. Without a telegraph or railroad, he had to rely on the irregular appearances of the steamships from San Francisco to receive news. Even newsprint supplies were erratic; a few issues of the *Herald* were printed on brown wrapping paper.

With profits dwindling, Ames decided in 1859 to try his luck in the rising Mormon community of San Bernardino. After printing a last issue of the *Herald* on April 7, 1860, Ames packed up his press and moved north to found the *San Bernardino Herald*. Tragically, only a few issues of the newspaper were printed before Ames died on July 28, 1861. There are no known surviving issues of this San Bernardino newspaper.

The nine-year run of the *San Diego Herald* nearly disappeared, as well. In 1901, San Diego pioneer E.W. Morse wrote to the San Diego Public Library and offered his complete run of the old newspaper, noting "there are no other copies of this celebrated publication in existence...the best and most appropriate place for [the *Herald*] is our own public library." Preserved and microfilmed by the library, copies of Ames's *Herald* continue to survive, providing an incomparable firsthand account of early San Diego.

SAN DIEGO'S HUMORIST: GEORGE HORATIO DERBY

We found ourselves in a large bar and billiard-room...Here I saw Lieutenant Derby, of the Topographical Engineers, an elderly gentlemen of emaciated appearance and serious cast of features. Constant study and unremitting attention to his laborious duties have reduced him almost to a skeleton...He was sent out from Washington some months since, "to dam the San Diego River," and he informed me, with a deep sigh and melancholy smile, he had done it (mentally) several times since his arrival.
—*from* Phoenixiana *(New York: D. Appleton and Company, 1855)*

The narrator of the passage above was the lieutenant himself. Young (and quite un-cmaciated, in fact) George Horatio Derby was an army engineer tasked with redirecting the channel of the San Diego River. The hapless

A painting of Lieutenant George Horatio Derby of the U.S. Topographical Engineers, based on a photograph taken in his West Point uniform. *Courtesy of Special Collections, San Diego Public Library.*

engineering project would be fodder for humor, from a man Mark Twain would call "the first great modern humorist."

Born in Massachusetts in 1823, Derby was a West Point graduate and veteran of the U.S.-Mexican War. He came west in 1849 as an officer for the Department of the Pacific. In the next four years, he would excel in survey and engineering projects in the Sacramento Valley and on the Colorado River.

In leisure hours, he contributed witty anecdotes to the *San Francisco Herald* under his West Point nickname, "Squibob." When the popular bits of satire attracted a rival using the same pen name in a competing newspaper, Derby "killed off" Squibob in a humorous obituary and adopted a new pseudonym: "John Phoenix."

Derby came to San Diego in January 1853. He found the town "pleasantly situated" on the banks of the San Diego River, with "perhaps, a hundred houses, some of wood, but mostly of the 'Adoban' or 'Gresan' order of architecture."

San Diego had a population of about seven hundred at the time, "two-thirds of whom are 'native and to the manner born,'" Derby observed. "The rest were a mixture of American, English, German, Hebrew, and Pike County." In "Sandyago—A Soliquy," Derby would pen: "The natives is all sorts complected; Some white, some black, & some kinder speckled."

Like many new arrivals in San Diego, the lieutenant's observations included comments on the town's notorious fleas. Derby's "feelings of indignation against those wretched insects" would result in his famed "Antidote for Fleas": "Boil a quart of tar until it becomes quite thin. Remove the clothing, and before the tar becomes perfectly cool, with a broad flat brush, apply a thin, smooth coating to the entire surface of the body and limbs. While the tar remains soft the flea becomes entangled in its tenacious folds, and is rendered perfectly harmless."

Vermin notwithstanding, Derby saw promise in the young town. The possibility of a transcontinental railroad terminating in San Diego "was within the range of probability," he decided. "The landholders about here are well aware of this fact, and consequently affix already incredible prices to very unprepossessing pieces of land." For himself, Derby claimed, "At present I should prefer the money to the real estate."

Derby's army assignment in San Diego was to redirect the San Diego River from the harbor—where it had been dumping silt into San Diego Bay—into False Bay (today's Mission Bay). To protect the value of the harbor to shipping, the army wanted to restore the river's "proper" outlet to the sea. Beyond the engineering challenge, the task was frustrated by poor funding. But the job did afford Derby lots of free time while he waited for money and direction from Washington.

Articles from "John Phoenix" began to appear in San Diego's newspaper, the *Herald*, published by Derby's good friend, John Judson Ames. When

Derby caricatured himself as the editor of the *Herald. From* Phoenixiana; or, Sketches and Burlesques *(1903).*

Ames left for San Francisco on a lengthy business trip in the summer of 1853, he made Derby the acting editor.

Derby produced six remarkable issues of the *Herald*, enlivening the columns with witty commentary and satire. His last issue—entitled the *Illustrated San Diego Herald*—featured comical woodcuts of current events. For a time, he changed the political stance of the *Herald* from Democrat to Whig and nearly pushed the Whig candidate for governor, William Waldo, to victory.

When the return of Ames was imminent, Derby printed the story of his "battle" with the offended editor: "We held [Ames] down over the press by our nose (which we had inserted between his teeth for that purpose) and while our hair was employed in holding one of his hands, we held the other in our left and…shouted to him, 'Say Waldo!'" Actually, Ames ignored the prank but noted, "Phoenix has played the 'devil' during our absence."

The editor encouraged his friend to publish his writings in a book. Derby was uninterested but eventually allowed Ames to sell the collection in New York City to D. Appleton and Company for $450. Ames apparently pocketed the money, and Derby never profited from the success of *Phoenixiana, Or, Sketches and Burlesques,* by "John Phoenix," which would be reprinted at least twenty times by 1890.

Derby left San Diego in 1855. (The unfinished "Derby Dike" on the San Diego River would wash away two years later. A permanent levee was not completed until 1876.) A difficult road building job followed in Oregon and Washington, where Derby observed that "it rains incessantly twenty-six hours a day for seventeen months of the year."

"We held [Ames] down over the press by our nose."
From Phoenixiana; or, Sketches and Burlesques *(1903)*.

Poor health plagued him the late 1850s. Under a doctor's care in New York City in August 1860, Derby complained in a letter to a friend in San Francisco about his prescribed meals: "Now you may imagine I lose flesh on this [diet] weighing 142 lbs. I am pleased with this result as I shall shortly exhibit myself at Barnum's Museum as the Living Skeleton and make a handsome fortune as Barnum as promised me $30.00 a week when I get down to 30 lbs in weight. It won't be long."

George Derby passed away eleven months later, at the age of thirty-eight, leaving a wife and three children. His collection of stories in *Phoenixiana* still stands as a classic of American humor.

HARRY HOUDINI COMES TO SAN DIEGO

A vaudeville act that is without its equal in the world today has been secured for the Grand theater…Harry Houdini, the noted handcuff and jail breaker, will give exhibitions of his skill here.
—San Diego Union, *October 5, 1907*

In the fall of 1907, Harry Houdini, soon to be known as the world's greatest magician and escape artist, came to San Diego to display his skills before crowded theater audiences. It was the era of vaudeville in America, and Houdini was a rising star in the popular variety entertainment field.

At age thirty-three, Houdini was a show business veteran, but fame had come slowly. After years of meager success as a magician in dime museums and circus sideshows, he began experimenting with escape stunts in the late 1890s. Following a triumphant tour of Europe in 1900, he returned to America as a proven escape artist, able to defeat any form of confinement, including handcuffs, leg irons, jail cells and straitjackets.

Touring with the popular Orpheum vaudeville circuit, Houdini came to Southern California in September 1907. A successful three-week tour in Los Angeles made him "the talk of the northern city." A new act featured a challenge from the U.S. Postal Service. Mail officials secured Houdini in an oversized leather mail pouch fastened with government padlocks. The escape artist quickly foiled the locks and escaped, in full view of the audience.

A more spectacular feat was performed outdoors before an estimated five thousand spectators. With his legs in chains and his hands manacled behind him, Houdini leaped from the roof of a pavilion into the reservoir of Westlake Park (known today as McArthur Park). After two minutes of

"The Handcuff King" Harry Houdini in 1905. *From McManus-Young Collection, Library of Congress.*

suspense, Houdini bobbed to the surface, free of his shackles.

A similar stunt was promised for San Diego, when the newspapers announced that the "Handcuff King" was coming to the city for a three-night engagement at the Grand Theatre on Fifth Street. Advertising proclaimed that Houdini, "absolutely the greatest act in vaudeville today," would "dive, handcuffed, from top of Spreckels' bunkers" into San Diego Bay at the foot of G Street.

The Houdini show at the Grand began on Monday night, October 7. In addition to the star attraction, the show offered "the usual good bill of vaudeville." The warm-up acts included a "clever monologist" who sang and told jokes; a "champion trumpeter" who drew applause for his patriotic numbers; and music and comedy from the Gilman sisters.

Following the other performers, Houdini took the stage for a one-hour performance. Before a sellout crowd, he began his act by demonstrating how simple handcuff escapes were performed. He then invited a committee of local police and county officials to take part in his show.

Police Chief William Neely and three of his officers, along with the district attorney, Lewis Kirby, and several county officials, mounted the stage. Using San Diego police property, "they manacled the magician hand and foot with cuffs, leg irons and shackles of every description then guarded the tiny cabinet in which he released himself." It took Houdini six minutes to free himself of every shackle.

Houdini concluded his show with the "stellar act of the evening," a straitjacket escape in full view of the theater audience. Four policemen strapped the jacket on and "exhorted themselves to the upmost in drawing up all of the buckles as tight as they could be drawn." As the audience shouted, "He'll never get out of that" and "They've got him now," Houdini writhed and twisted until

THE GRAND THEATRE

Monday, Tuesday and Wednesday,

OCT. 7, 8 and 9,

HARRY HOUDINI

King of Handcuff
and Jail Breakers

Absolutely the greatest act in vaudeville today. Direct from Orpheum circuit.

Will dive, handcuffed, from top of Spreckels' bunkers Monday afternoon at 4 o'clock.

Prices—50c, 75c, $1.00 and $1.50.

San Diego's Grand Theatre on Fifth Street featured Harry Houdini, "the greatest act in vaudeville," for three days in October 1907. San Diego Union, *October 8, 1907.*

he managed to raise his hands above his head and unfasten the buckles. "An uproar of applause greeted him as he threw the jacket from him."

For the final night of the engagement, Houdini invited four employees of Marston's department store to nail him in a shipping case and then nail ropes around it. As usual, the magician escaped with apparent ease.

Regrettably, Houdini left town without performing the advertised underwater escape in San Diego Bay. For reasons unknown (or at least unreported), the plan for a handcuffed Houdini to jump from Spreckels' wharf into the bay never occurred.

In the next few years, the fame of Harry Houdini grew quickly as his escape acts became more challenging and death defying. He became the highest-paid act in vaudeville and eventually created his own, hugely successful evening show. Houdini never performed again in San Diego and died on Halloween in 1926, of acute peritonitis, at age fifty-two.

THE EVANGELIST AND THE MUCKRAKER

When Aimee dived into the Pacific Ocean and emerged on the Mexican desert, thus performing a feat which will not be duplicated until babies grow on walnut trees, she reckoned that the rest of the world was as foolish as she.
—San Diego Herald, *July 29, 1926*

The apparent drowning death of famed evangelist Aimee Semple McPherson off the coast of Santa Monica in 1926 shocked the world. Even more stunning was her reappearance weeks later in the Sonora desert. The sensational story she told of her kidnapping and miraculous escape spawned front-page news coverage that lasted for months.

One of the most widely read observers of the McPherson mystery was a seventy-five-year-old newsman from San Diego: Abraham R. Sauer, editor and publisher of the weekly *San Diego Herald*. Sauer's mocking and inflammatory explanation of the revered preacher's adventure would lead to his prosecution in federal court and test the limits of free speech.

Abraham R. Sauer, editor and publisher of the weekly *San Diego Herald. San Diego History Center.*

San Diego's radical newsman was born in Marine City, Michigan. As a young man, he joined the gold rush to the Black Hills of the Dakota Territory and then moved to Nebraska and learned newspaper work on the *Omaha Daily Bee*. He moved to San Diego in the 1890s and acquired the *Herald*. Sauer would turn the *Herald* into a provocative medium for personal journalism that attacked the local political establishment at every opportunity. He treated San Diegans to headlines such as "Brainless Mayor and Spineless Council Take Orders from Greedy Merchants" and "Is the Press to Be Muzzled, Or Truth a Crime?"

Bible in hand, Aimee Semple
McPherson posed for the
camera, February 14, 1927.
*National Photo Company
Collection, Library of Congress.*

Not surprisingly, the defaming editor was hauled into court repeatedly on charges of slandering the rich and powerful. He would be sued eighteen times for libel—winning each case. But his July 29, 1926 edition of the *Herald*, which covered the McPherson affair in colorful detail, nearly landed him in prison.

Even without the Sauer touch, the story was sensational enough. "Sister Aimee," age thirty-five, famed Canadian-born preacher of the "Foursquare Gospel," had disappeared on May 18 while swimming at a deserted beach at Ocean Park in Santa Monica. Her secretary would recall waving to the preacher as she entered the water. But she failed to return—"a victim of the breakers," everyone assumed.

That night, Aimee's mother, Mrs. Minnie "Mother" Kennedy, confirmed the tragedy to a shocked congregation at McPherson's church, the Angelus Temple, in Los Angeles. "We know she is with Jesus," she told the tearful crowd. "Pray for her." Donations were then gathered as a memorial, eventually totaling about $36,000.

Five weeks later, in the early morning of June 23, McPherson reappeared. Found in Agua Prieta, Mexico, across the border from Douglas, Arizona, the evangelist told rescuers a harrowing story of her kidnapping, torture and dramatic escape from a shack in the desert.

On her return to Los Angeles, Sister Aimee received a triumphal welcome home. Thirty thousand people greeted her train at Union

Station and then followed her car to the Angelus Temple, where she thanked her devoted followers.

But soon doubters began to question McPherson's story of abduction. Why did she reappear in unblemished street clothes when she had last been "seen" wearing a swimsuit? Why did her grass-stained shoes show no evidence of her claimed thirteen-hour trek through the desert? Worse, witnesses began to appear who recalled seeing her in late May in the coastal town of Carmel accompanied by Kenneth Ormiston, a former church employee who had gone missing at the same time as McPherson.

None of the news stories showed more scorn and irreverence toward the evangelist and her followers than Abraham Sauer's front page of the *Herald*. "She had staged the perfect disappearance," Sauer wrote. "A conniving secretary had aided and abetted her. Her moronic and purblind followers had swallowed hook, line and sinker."

"As the world now knows," the editor judged, "her mother did the ballyhooing while her daughter did the cooing, and while Aimee was being satisfied at Carmel-by-the Sea Mother Kennedy was filling the treasure chest in the City of the Angels."

Sauer's account was a best seller. Copies of the *Herald* were mailed far and wide. A post office worker would later testify in court that he shipped bundles of the four-page newspaper weighing nearly forty pounds each. The single issue sold for one dollar a copy in New York City.

But the lurid description of Aimee's "ten days in a love shack" was too much for the U.S. postal inspector in Los Angeles. On August 13, Sauer was charged with sending obscene literature through the mails. At his arraignment, defense attorneys argued that the article was "based upon truth," with the editor justifiably criticizing McPherson "for conduct not becoming to her teachings."

The case went to trial the next month. After one federal jury deadlocked, Sauer was retried. He was acquitted on October 16.

Others were less fortunate. A Los Angeles judge fined four newsstand vendors $100 each after convictions for selling the "obscene" newspaper. Harry Turner, the hapless publisher of the St. Louis magazine *Much Ado*, was sentenced to two years in Leavenworth Federal Prison for reprinting and mailing the now-notorious July 29 edition of the *Herald*.

While Sauer was defending himself in court, the scandal over Sister Aimee's month-long disappearance grew. A skeptical Los Angeles district attorney charged her with obstruction of justice in September but, lacking hard evidence, dismissed the case before it reached trial.

On October 26, 1927, with her reputation on the mend, McPherson came to San Diego to preach before a packed auditorium at San Diego High School. Three nights of revival meetings followed. "Well, Aimee the Delectable is here," editor Sauer caustically observed. "Even the memories of her historic dip into the Pacific and her consequent cavorting…have gone from the mind."

Aimee Semple McPherson would continue her ministry into the 1940s, though questions about the mysterious "kidnapping" haunted her reputation. She died on September 26, 1944, from an overdose of barbiturates—an accident, according to the report from the coroner.

FRANK "BRING 'EM BACK ALIVE" BUCK

Frank H. Buck, one of the foremost zoological collectors of the United States, arrived yesterday from San Francisco and at once assumed the duties of his position as director of the San Diego zoo. Under his direction, the splendid zoo here is expected to increase rapidly in size and reputation.
—San Diego Union, *June 14, 1923*

The adventures of Frank "Bring 'Em Back Alive" Buck captivated millions of people throughout the world in the 1930s and '40s. Celebrated to this day for his exploits as a wild animal hunter and trader, Buck is less well known for his brief, tumultuous tenure as director of the San Diego Zoo.

Frank Buck was the zoo's first full-time, salaried director. Signed by the Zoological Society to a three-year contract that paid $4,000 annually, the forty-one-year-old Buck came to San Diego backed by the strong recommendation of Dr. William T. Hornaday, director of the famed Bronx Zoo.

He started work in June 1923, voicing excitement for his new job to reporters. "We have the best zoo west of Chicago," Buck boasted, "and we are going to make it even bigger and better." He began with an ambitious building program, constructing new exhibit cages for birds and monkeys and acquiring new animals for the growing collection.

But his efforts were not appreciated by the board of the Zoological Society, particularly its president and founder of the zoo, Dr. Harry M. Wegeforth. A strong-willed, hands-on president, Wegeforth walked the zoo grounds daily and immediately clashed with the independent-minded Buck. After only three months, the zoo board fired Buck, charging that the man "could not be trusted."

Successful big game collector and failed zoo curator Frank Buck. *From Buck's autobiography* All in a Lifetime *(New York: Robert M. McBride Company, 1941).*

Buck decided to sue the Zoological Society and Dr. Wegeforth, for breach of contract. Claiming that he had given up his lucrative animal-collecting business to work in San Diego and suffered injury to his reputation, Buck sought damages of $22,500.

In his court deposition, Buck cited a litany of grievances, most of them focused on the actions of Wegeforth. Buck claimed the zoo president had interfered with "practically everything" and had conspired with the board to "belittle and disparage" his efforts as director. He had been fired, Buck believed, after he built a new bird enclosure without personal authorization from Wegeforth.

He also made surprising allegations about Wegeforth. A professional physician, Wegeforth took a strong interest in veterinary medicine and personally monitored the health of the animals. But Buck charged that the doctor had killed a sick tiger by dosing the animal with calomel and had been responsible for the deaths of 150 snakes that had been force-fed with a sausage stuffer.

Quite a different story emerged in court from the testimony of board member Thomas N. Faulconer and several others. All witnesses flatly denied Buck's charge that snakes had been killed by force-feeding, and they suggested the sick tiger had died after a suspicious blow to the head.

According to these witnesses, Buck's problems stemmed from his unwillingness to consult with the board on everyday policy. Frequently, he deliberately defied board directives. "The whole character of the man," Wegeforth testified, "was insubordination."

There was more involved than a clash of wills. Wegeforth charged that Buck was incompetent. Business deals with other zoos or animal collectors were mismanaged and undocumented. On one occasion, Buck had ordered new nameplates for animal cages and pens. The order had to be returned when it was found that half of the names had been misspelled by Buck.

Wegeforth also cited examples of Buck's failure to recognize disease or properly care for sick animals. He replied to the charge that snakes had died by saying that Buck himself had mistreated the reptiles: "Mr. Buck stuffed down, by the most inhuman way of feeding, snake meat down the throat of a boa constrictor instead of using a more modern method of stomach tube or feeding the meat through a tube."

The final straw was an incident involving the zoo's two Indian elephants, Empress and Queenie. Buck believed that the hides of the elephants, which appeared dry and cracked, would benefit from "oiling," a customary practice that Dr. Wegeforth learned often caused pneumonia or kidney disease.

Despite the president's orders, Buck oiled the elephants. Wegeforth recalled, "They quickly became piteous-looking creatures, their trunks grew flaccid and seemed about a foot longer than usual, and their abdomens almost touched the ground. I was afraid they were doomed." Fortunately, Empress and Queenie recovered. Frank Buck, however, was sacked.

On February 20, 1924, superior court judge Charles Andrews ruled against the plaintiff Buck and ordered him to pay court costs of twenty-four dollars. He soon left San Diego and resumed his career as a "zoological collector."

In 1930, Buck became a bestselling author with his book *Bring 'Em Back Alive*. The film documentary that followed made him an international star.

He returned to San Diego in 1943. Lecturing in the Russ auditorium of San Diego High School, the world-famous adventurer recounted his thirty years as a hunter of wild animals. Buck "brought gasps" from the audience as he described his breathtaking struggles in the jungle with venomous cobras, screaming leopards and man-eating tigers. His brief misadventures at the San Diego Zoo, twenty years earlier, were long forgotten.

Buck's 1941 autobiography, *All in a Lifetime*, would not mention his lawsuit against the San Diego Zoo. But interestingly, "while acting as temporary director of the San Diego Zoo," he claimed credit for inventing a method for force-feeding snakes—the means, he would boast, "by which captive pythons are mainly fed today."

SOURCES

A FRONTIER PORT

The Battle of San Diego Bay

Bancroft, Hubert Howe. *History of California*. Vol. II. Santa Barbara, CA: Wallace Hebberd, 1966.

Cleveland, Richard J. *Voyage of a Merchant Navigator*. New York: Harper & Brothers, 1886.

Richman, Irving Berdine. *California under Spain and Mexico, 1535–1847*. Boston: Houghton Mifflin, 1911.

Shaler, William. *Journal of a Voyage Between China and the Northwestern Coast of America: Made in 1804*. Claremont, CA: Saunders Studio Press, 1935.

Richard H. Dana Discovers the Best Harbor on the Coast

Bancroft, Hubert Howe. *History of California*. Vol. III. Santa Barbara, CA: Wallace Hebberd, 1966.

Dana, Richard Henry, Jr. *Two Years Before the Mast: A Personal Narrative of Life at Sea*. Los Angeles: Ward Ritchie Press, 1964.

Smythe, William E. *History of San Diego, 1542–1908*. San Diego, CA: History Company, 1908.

War Comes to the Pueblo

DuPont, Samuel Francis. *Extracts from Private Journal—Letters of Captain S.F. DuPont, while in Command of the Cyane during the War with Mexico, 1846–1848*. Wilmington, DE: Ferris Bros., Printers, 1885.

———. *Official Dispatches and Letters of Rear Admiral DuPont, U.S. Navy, 1846–48, 1861–63*. Wilmington, DE: Ferris Brothers, 1883.

Harlow, Neal. *California Conquered: War and Peace on the Pacific, 1846–1850*. Berkeley: University of California Press, 1982.

Merrill, James M. *DuPont, The Making of an Admiral: A Biography of Samuel Francis DuPont*. New York: Dodd, Mead & Company, 1986.

Smythe, William E. *History of San Diego, 1542–1908*. San Diego, CA: History Company, 1908.

The Davis Folly

Davis, William Heath. *Seventy-five Years in California*. San Francisco, CA: John Howell, 1929.

Harlow, Neal. *Maps of the Pueblo Lands of San Diego: 1602–1874*. Los Angeles: Dawson's Book Shop, 1987.

Rolle, Andrew F. *An American in California: The Biography of William Heath Davis, 1822–1909*. San Marino, CA: Huntington Library, 1956.

Smythe, William E. *History of San Diego, 1542–1908*. San Diego, CA: History Company, 1908.

A Library for San Diego

Breed, Clara E. *Turning the Pages: San Diego Public Library History, 1882–1982*. San Diego, CA: Friends of the San Diego Public Library, 1983.

Hensley, Herbert C. "Early San Diego: Reminiscences of Early Days and People." Undated typescript. Special Collections, San Diego Public Library.

Smythe, William E. *History of San Diego, 1542–1908*. San Diego, CA: History Company, 1908.

BUILDING A CITY

The Great Boom of the Eighties

Dumke, Glenn S. *The Boom of the Eighties in Southern California*. San Marino, CA: Huntington Library, 1944.

San Diego Union, 1887–88.

Smith, Walter Gifford. *The Story of San Diego*. San Diego, CA: City Printing Company, 1892.

Smythe, William E. *History of San Diego, 1542–1908*. San Diego, CA: History Company, 1908.

Van Dyke, Theodore S. *Millionaires of a Day: An Inside History of the Great Southern California "Boom."* New York: Fords, Howard & Hulbert, 1890.

The Telephone Comes to San Diego

An Illustrated History of Southern California. Chicago: Lewis Publishing Company, 1890.

Los Angeles Times.

San Diego Union.

Smythe, William E. *History of San Diego, 1542–1908*. San Diego, CA: History Company, 1908.

Thompson, John Waldo. *Memoirs, 1842–1932*. Typescript. San Diego History Center.

The Sewering of the City

Kelly, Michael, MD, ed. "First Annual Report of the Board of Health of the City of San Diego for the Year Ending December 31ˢᵗ, 1888." *Journal of San Diego History* 48 (Fall 2002).

Melosi, Martin V. *The Sanitary City: Urban Infrastructure in America from Colonial Times to the Present*. Baltimore, MD: Johns Hopkins Press, 2000.

San Diego Union, 1886–89.

Smythe, William E. *History of San Diego, 1542–1908*. San Diego, CA: History Company, 1908.

Waring, George E., Jr. "The Sewerage of San Diego." *Sewerage and Land-Drainage*. 3ʳᵈ ed. New York: D. Van Nostrand Company, 1891.

A Floating Forest to Build a City

Allen, Alice Benson. *Simon Benson: Northwest Lumber King*. Portland, OR: Binford & Mort Publishers, 1971.

"History of the Robertson Log Raft." *The Timberman* (January 1929).

San Diego Tribune.

San Diego Union.

The House Movers

"House-Moving." *American Agriculturist* (November 1873).

An Illustrated History of Southern California. Chicago: Lewis Publishing Company, 1890.

"John D. and Ida Palmer." *San Diego County Pioneer Families*. San Diego Historical Society, 1977.

San Diego County, Superior Court. *T. West, Jr. v. J.D. Palmer, et al*. Case no. 7185. San Diego History Center.

San Diego Union.

Stewart, Don M. *Frontier Port: A Chapter in San Diego's History*. Los Angeles: W. Ritchie Press, 1965.

LAW AND DISORDER

The Bloody River Crossing on the Colorado

"Estate of John C. Glanton." Fort Yuma, Documents File #2. San Diego County Law Library.

Guinn, J.M. "Yuma Depredations and the Glanton War." *Publications of the Historical Society of Southern California* (1903).

Harris, Benjamin Butler. *The Gila Trail*. Norman: University of Oklahoma Press, 1960.

Hayes, Benjamin. *Emigrant Notes: San Diego, Calif., 1875. ms.* (microfilm). Bancroft Library, University of California–Berkeley.

Martin, Douglas D. *Yuma Crossing*. Albuquerque: University of New Mexico, 1954.

"Our Kin: Descendants of Joshua Lincoln…of Taunton, Massachusetts." HeritageQuest Online. persi.heritagequestonline.com

"Persifer F. Smith to Captain Irvin McDowell," May 25, 1850. 31 Congress 2nd Session, Senate Ex Doc. 1 pt. 2.

Stanford, Leland G. *San Diego's Legal Lore, & the Bar: History of Law and Justice in San Diego County.* San Diego, CA: Law Library Justice Foundation, 1968.

Sweeney, Thomas W. "Military Occupation of California, 1849–53." From the *Journal of Lieutenant Thomas W. Sweeny.* Reprinted from the *Journal of the Military Service Institution,* 1909.

Woodward, Arthur. *Feud on the Colorado.* Los Angeles: Westernlore Press, 1955.

Jailbreak

Daily San Diegan, April 1888.

San Diego Sun, April 1888.

San Diego Tribune, April 1888.

San Diego Union, 1884–88.

San Quentin case file for Theodore Fowler. California State Archives, Sacramento.

The Carnegie Library Art Robbery

Los Angeles Herald, March 1909.

Los Angeles Times, February–April 1909.

San Diego Sun, February–April 1909.

San Diego Tribune, February–April 1909.

San Diego Union, February–April 1909.

Mutiny on the Dudhope

Gray, Edwyn A. *The Killing Time: The U-boat War, 1914–18.* New York: Charles Scribner's Sons, 1972.

MacMullen, Jerry. *They Came by Sea: A Pictorial History of San Diego Bay.* San Diego, CA: Maritime Museum Association, 1988.

Messimer, Dwight. *Berschollen: World War I U-Boat Losses.* Annapolis, MD: Naval Institute Press, 2002.

San Diego Tribune, December 1914.

San Diego Union, November–December 1914.

Shootout in Downtown

Castanien, Pliny. *To Protect and Serve: A History of the San Diego Police Department and Its Chiefs, 1889–1989*. San Diego, CA: San Diego Historical Society, 1993.

Los Angeles Times. "The Angry Life of Robert Page Anderson." February 27, 1972.

———. "I Wish I Never Got Off that Bus." April 3, 1990.

San Diego Union, April–June 1965.

WATER FOR A THIRSTY REGION

The Engineering Marvel of Sweetwater Dam

Fowler, Lloyd Charles. "A History of the Dams and Water Supply of Western San Diego County." Master's thesis. University of California–Berkeley, 1953.

San Diego Union, April 1888.

Savage, Hiram N. "Flood Overflow of the Sweetwater Dam." *Engineering News-Record* 34 (August 15, 1895).

Schulyer, James Dix. *Reservoirs for Irrigation, Water-Power and Domestic Water-Supply*. New York: John Wiley & Sons, 1909.

"The Sweetwater Dam." *Engineering News* 20 (October 1888).

Trook, Leslie. *100 Years of "Sweet Water."* Chula Vista, CA: Sweetwater Authority, 1988.

The Rainmaker

Fowler, Lloyd Charles. "A History of the Dams and Water Supply of Western San Diego County." Master's thesis. University of California–Berkeley, 1953.

Hatfield, Charles M. *Charles M. Hatfield Collection*. Special Collections, San Diego Public Library.

Higgins, Shelley J. *This Fantastic City, San Diego*. San Diego, CA: City of San Diego, 1956.

San Diego Union, January 1916.

Wooden Pipes to the City

"Condition of Wood-Stave Pipe on Reclamation Projects." *Engineering News-Record* (March 23, 1922).

Ledoux, J.W. "Some Observations Concerning Wood Pipe." *Journal of the American Water Works Association* 9 (July 1922).

San Diego Union, 1901–2, 1905–6.

Savage, Hiram N. *Feature History, Otay Reservoir (San Diego Second Main Line)*. City of San Diego, 1931.

Wiley, Herbert M. *Irrigation Engineering*. New York: John Wiley & Sons, 1909.

A Dam Fiasco

Fowler, Lloyd Charles. "A History of the Dams and Water Supply of Western San Diego County." Master's thesis. University of California–Berkeley, 1953.

Higgins, Shelley J. *This Fantastic City, San Diego*. San Diego, CA: City of San Diego, 1956.

Los Angeles Times, 1927–28.

"Report of Caretaker, City Engineer's Camp." September 20, 1929. *Sutherland Dam Feature History*. Vol. 1. City of San Diego.

San Diego Union, 1927–32.

Savage, Hiram N. *San Dieguito Project: Sutherland Reservoir Dam Feature*. City of San Diego, 1927.

"Sutherland Dam for San Diego Water Supply." *Western Construction News* 10 (January 1927).

"25-Yr. Old Sutherland Dam Being Completed by San Diego." *Western Construction News* 27 (November 1952).

Damming Mission Gorge

Higgins, Shelley J. *This Fantastic City, San Diego*. San Diego, CA: City of San Diego, 1956.

"Hiram Newton Savage." Inventory of the Hiram Newton Savage Papers, 1905–1933. Online Archive of California. www.oac.cdlib.org.

Los Angeles Times, 1928.

Melbourne, Robert E. "San Diego's Water Crusader, Fred A. Heilbron." *Journal of San Diego History* 32 (Fall 1986).

San Diego Sun, November 1930.

San Diego Tribune, November 1930.
San Diego Union, June 1923, November–December 1930.

THE NOTORIOUS STINGAREE

Liquor, Guns and "Russian Mike"

Los Angeles Times, March–April 1899.
San Diego County, "Coroner's Inquest on Daniel Cavanaugh," March 27, 1899. San Diego History Center.
San Diego Union, March–May 1899.
San Quentin case file for Michael Rose. California State Archives, Sacramento.

Policing the City

Alta California. "The Evils of Stud-Horse Poker." July 4, 1884.
Castanien, Pliny. *To Protect and Serve: A History of the San Diego Police Department and Its Chiefs, 1889–1989*. San Diego, CA: San Diego Historical Society, 1993.
San Diego Union, 1887–88.
Willard, Steve. *San Diego Police Department*. Charleston, SC: Arcadia Publishing, 2007.

The People v. Breedlove

Castanien, Pliny. *To Protect and Serve: A History of the San Diego Police Department and Its Chiefs, 1889–1989*. San Diego. CA: San Diego Historical Society, 1993.
Hensley, Herbert C. "Early San Diego: Reminiscences of Early Days and People." Undated typescript. Special Collections, San Diego Public Library.
Los Angeles Times, July 1891.
San Diego County. "Coroner's Inquest on Joseph R. Brown, July 15, 1891." San Diego History Center.
San Diego Sun, July 1891.
San Diego Union, July–October 1891

Till Burnes's Saloon

An Illustrated History of Southern California. Chicago: Lewis Publishing Company, 1890.

San Diego County, Superior Court. *County of San Diego v. Till A. Burnes.* Case no. 3943. San Diego History Center.

San Diego Union, 1869–89.

Raid on the Red-Light District

Higgins, Shelley J. *This Fantastic City, San Diego.* San Diego, CA: City of San Diego, 1956.

MacPhail, Elizabeth C. "When the Red Lights Went Out in San Diego." *Journal of San Diego History* 20 (Spring 1974).

McKanna, Clare V., Jr. "Prostitutes, Progressives, and Police: The Viability of Vice in San Diego, 1900–1930." *Journal of San Diego History* 35 (Winter 1989).

San Diego Union, 1912.

WINGS OVER SAN DIEGO

An Airship or a Lead Balloon?

Articles of Incorporation of the Toliver Aerial Navigation Company. No. 2521. San Diego History Center.

Mills, James. "Dread Dirigible of Golden Hill." *San Diego and Point Magazine* (October–November 1958).

New York Times, May 1912.

San Diego Union, 1910–11.

Charles Lindbergh Takes Flight

Berg, A. Scott. *Lindbergh.* New York: G.P. Putnam's, 1998.

"Destination Paris." *Union-Title Topics* (March–April 1957).

Morrow, Ed. Interview with Robert Wright, June 2, 1974. San Diego History Center.

Owen, Grace Arlington. "Creative Reference Work." *Wilson Library Bulletin* (September 1932).

San Diego Union, 1927.

Ruth Alexander: Pioneer of the Air

New York Times, July–September 1930.

San Diego Sun, March–September 1930.

San Diego Union, 1929–30.

Scott, Mary L. *San Diego: Air Capital of the West*. Virginia Beach, VA: Donning Co., 2005.

America's First Airline

Pescador, Katrina, and Alan Renga. *Aviation in San Diego*. Charleston, SC: Arcadia Publishing, 2007.

San Diego Tribune, March 1925.

San Diego Union, March 1925.

Wagner, William. *Ryan, the Aviator: Being the Adventures & Ventures of Pioneer Airman & Businessman, T. Claude Ryan*. New York: McGraw-Hill Book Company, 1971.

A SPORTING CITY

Seabiscuit v. Ligaroti

Hillenbrand, Laura. *Seabiscuit: An American Legend*. New York: Random House, 2001.

Holtzclaw, Kenneth M., and the Del Mar Thoroughbred Club. *Del Mar Racetrack*. Charleston, SC: Arcadia Publishing, 2006.

Los Angeles Times, August 12, 1988.

Murray, William. *Del Mar: It's Life & Good Times*. Del Mar, CA: Del Mar Thoroughbred Club, 1988.

San Diego Sun, August 1938.

San Diego Union, August 1938.

Westgate Park: Home of the Padres

Britton, James. "Mission Valley." *San Diego Magazine* (January 1957).

San Diego Union, February–April 1958.

Swank, Bill. *Baseball in San Diego: From the Padres to Petco*. Charleston, SC: Arcadia Publishing, 2004.

The Chargers Come to San Diego

San Diego Union, December 1960–October 1961.

Tobias, Todd. *Charging Through the AFL: Los Angeles and San Diego Chargers Football in the 1960s.* Nashville, TN: Turner Publishing, 2004.

A Floating Stadium on Mission Bay

Hope, Frank L., and Associates. "San Diego All-American Stadium, Phase 2 Report: Prepared for the City of San Diego." 1965.

San Diego Union, October 1964–April 1965.

Western Management Consultants, Inc. "Economic Feasibility of the Proposed All-American Stadium for San Diego." 1964.

SAN DIEGANS TO REMEMBER

The Newspaperman

Dawson, Muir. *History and Bibliography of Southern California Newspapers, 1851–1876.* Los Angeles: Dawson's Book Shop, 1950.

"E.W. Morse to Board of Library Trustees," February 13, 1901. Minutes of the Board of Library Trustees. Special Collections, San Diego Public Library.

Phoenix, John [pseud. of George H. Derby]. *Phoenixiana; or, Sketches and Burlesques.* New York: D. Appleton and Company, 1903.

San Diego Herald, May 29, 1851.

Smythe, William E. *History of San Diego, 1542–1908.* San Diego, CA: History Company, 1908.

San Diego's Humorist: George Horatio Derby

Ciruzzi, Canice G. "Phoenix Revisited: Another Look at George Horatio Derby." *Journal of San Diego History* 26 (Spring 1980).

Reynolds, Richard Derby, ed. *Squibob: An Early California Humorist.* San Francisco: Squibob Press, 1990.

Stewart, George R. *John Phoenix, Esq., The Veritable Squibob. A Life of Captain George H. Derby, U.S.A.* New York: H. Holt and Company, 1937.

Harry Houdini Comes to San Diego

Los Angeles Herald, September–October 1907.
San Diego Sun, October 1907.
San Diego Tribune, October 1907.
San Diego Union, October 1907.
San Francisco Call, September 1907.

The Evangelist and the Muckraker

Higgins, Shelley J. *This Fantastic City, San Diego*. San Diego, CA: City of San Diego, 1956.

Lately, Thomas. *The Vanishing Evangelist: The Aimee Semple McPherson Kidnapping Affair*. New York: Viking Press, 1959.

Los Angeles Times, May–October 1926.

McWilliams, Carey. "Aimee Semple McPherson: 'Sunlight in My Soul.'" In *The Aspirin Age, 1919–1941*. New York: Simon and Schuster, 1949.

Pierce, J. Kingston. "The Abduction of Aimee." *American History* (February 2000).

San Diego Union, May–October 1926.

San Diego Weekly Herald, July 1926.

Frank "Bring 'Em Back Alive" Buck

San Diego County, Superior Court. *Frank H. Buck v. Zoological Society of San Diego, a Corporation, and Harry M. Wegeforth*. Case no. 40,507.

San Diego Union, June 1923–February 1924.

Wegeforth, Harry Milton, MD, and Neil Morgan. *It Began With a Roar: The Story of San Diego's World-Famed Zoo*. San Diego, CA: Pioneer Printers, 1953.

INDEX

ABOUT THE AUTHOR

Richard Crawford is the supervisor of Special Collections at the San Diego Public Library. He is the former archives director at the San Diego Historical Society, where he also edited the *Journal of San Diego History* for nine years. Born in Long Beach in 1953, he has been a San Diegan since 1973. He has degrees in history (San Diego State University) and library science (San Jose State University). In his thirty-year career as a historian and archivist, he has written extensively on local history, including the book *Stranger Than Fiction: Vignettes of San Diego History* (1995) and over 170 articles for the *San Diego Union-Tribune* that provide the content for *The Way We Were in San Diego*.